CLIMBING THE MOUNTAIN

My Search for Meaning

G·K
Hall
&Co.

Also by Kirk Douglas
in Large Print:

The Ragman's Son: An Autobiography
Dance with the Devil
Last Tango in Brooklyn

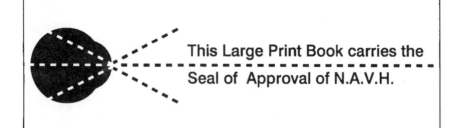

This Large Print Book carries the
Seal of Approval of N.A.V.H.

CLIMBING THE MOUNTAIN

My Search for Meaning

KIRK DOUGLAS

G.K. Hall & Co.
Thorndike, Maine

Published in 1998 by arrangement with Simon & Schuster, Inc.

G.K. Hall Large Print Nonfiction Series.

The text of this Large Print edition is unabridged. Other aspects of the book may vary from the original edition.

Set in 16 pt. Aldine 721.

Printed in the United States on permanent paper.

Library of Congress Catalog in Publication Data
Douglas, Kirk, 1916–
    Climbing the mountain : my search for meaning / Kirk Douglas.
        p.   cm.
    Originally published: New York : Simon & Schuster, 1997.
    ISBN 0-7838-8359-5 (lg. print : hc : alk. paper)
    1. Douglas, Kirk, 1916– . 2. Motion picture actors and actresses — United States — Biography. 3. Actors, Jewish — United States — Biography. 4. Large type books. I. Title.
    [PN2287.D54A3 1998]
    791.43'028'092—dc21
    [B]   97–41815

Acknowledgments

So many people help you in getting a book published that it is easy to forget some of the names. So, from the outset, I apologize to anyone I am about to overlook.

First of all, I must thank Michael Korda, editor-in-chief of Simon & Schuster, for responding with such enthusiasm to my scribblings. I must also thank all the people who did such a fine job through the many and varied aspects of the publication process: Chuck Adams, for his sensitive line editing; Andrew Hafitz, for his meticulous copy editing; Jane Centofante, for her thorough fact-checking; Jackie Seow, for her inspired cover design; Edith Fowler, for her eye-catching book design; Natalie Goldstein, for her painstaking photo research; Victoria Meyer and John Mooney, for their dedication to publicizing the book; and last, but certainly never least, Alan Nevins, my agent, for steering the whole ship to port.

Finally, how can I begin to thank Uriela Obst, Ushi, who has been my editor and guide through all my six books. I am indebted to her more than I can say.

To my past —
my mother, Bryna
my father, Harry

To my present —
my wife, Anne
my sons, Michael, Joel, Peter, Eric

To my future —
my grandchildren
Cameron, Kelsey, Tyler

"Don't aim at success — the more you aim at it and make it a target, the more you are going to miss it. For success, like happiness, cannot be pursued; it must ensue, and it only does so as the unintended side-effect of one's personal dedication to a cause greater than oneself or as the by-product of one's surrender to a person other than oneself. Happiness must happen, and the same holds for success: you have to let it happen by not caring about it. I want you to listen to what your conscience commands you to do and go on to carry it out to the best of your knowledge. Then you will live to see that in the long run — in the long run, I say! — success will follow you precisely because you had forgotten to think about it."

VICTOR FRANKL
Man's Search for Meaning

CHAPTER

ONE

I'll never forget the date — February 13, 1991, the day before Valentine's Day — the most important day in my life, the day I met two young men who would change my life forever: Lee Manelski and David Tomlinson.

Lee Manelski, a handsome, virile guy, was forty-six, the same age as my son Michael. Lee was the son of a former Navy pilot and veteran captain with TWA. Like Michael, Lee followed in his father's footsteps. Learning to fly before he could drive a car, he became the youngest flight engineer to be hired by TWA.

But flying the huge TWA jets was tame stuff to Lee. Before long he had found a new challenge — aerobatics. This is figure skating in the sky — somersaults; loop-the-loops; flying upside down; spiraling down at breakneck speed, then spinning gracefully to climb the skies again in a gravity-defying vertical line.

In 1987, the year Michael won his second Oscar, Lee won his second National Aerobatics Championship, becoming the number-one ranked aerobatics pilot in the United States.

Now he used every free moment to prepare for the international championships and was flying more than ever, managing to squeeze in time to give lessons to promising new recruits.

That is how Lee met David Tomlinson. David was eighteen, the exact age as Lee's own son, and not too far off in age from my grandson, Cameron.

Tall, lean and wholesomely handsome in a *Leave It to Beaver* kind of way, David was crazy about flying. The son of a Continental Airlines pilot, David, like Lee, learned to fly a plane before he could drive. All David wanted to do was spend his time up in the sky. When David decided to learn aerobatic flying, his father suggested he learn from the country's best, Lee Manelski.

David was just the kind of enthusiastic and tal-

Left: U.S. aerobatics champion Lee Manelski, 46, doing his thing.
(© Rob St. John)
Right: David Tomlinson, 18, Lee's best student.
(Courtesy of the Tomlinson Family)

ented student that Lee loved. Within half a dozen lessons he had mastered flying upside down, a very hard thing to learn, as it disorients the pilot — lefts are rights, rights are lefts — who must think fast before the gravity-fed fuel stops flowing. By February, Lee was predicting that David was not only ready to enter his first competition to be held in June, but he was sure the boy would win the novice class hands down.

On that eventful day, February 13, 1991, David did the usual thing. He left his school, Thousand Oaks High, to drive to Santa Paula Airport — a tiny airport in the middle of orchard country about seventy-five miles north of Los Angeles — for his lesson. He'd have a long day before it was through — school, aerobatics lesson, and then on to a part-time job at the Moorepark Recreation Department. His plate was full. The school year was rapidly coming to an end. Already he'd had his graduation photo taken and was making plans for the prom. He was excited about starting college in the fall.

Lee too had a busy day planned. On his agenda was giving a lesson to David in "touch-and-go" landings. That night he would be delivering a lecture to amateur pilots at Camarillo Airport. The subject: aviation safety.

My day had also been full.

I had come up to Fillmore, the town next door to Santa Paula, to go over the notes for my third book — my novel to be called *The Gift* — with my editor, Ursula Obst.

11

Ursula — Ushi, as she is known to her friends — had been my editor ever since 1987, when she worked on my autobiography, *The Ragman's Son*. I loved going up to her tiny farm nestled between the Santa Susana and the Los Padres mountain ranges.

Rural Fillmore is a Garden of Eden, fragrant with the intoxicating smell of orange blossoms, alive with the vibrant green of citrus groves.

I enjoyed eating warm oranges plucked straight from a tree, I loved feeding the horses, and even shoveling the horse manure. It felt good to stroke the smooth hide of my horse Sport as he gave me a condescending shake of his head and went back to chomping his hay. This is the same feeling I had back in my childhood, when my father's horse Bill was unhitched from the wagon and I fed him hay, oats and water. The smell of hay, the sound of a horse loosening his lips, reminded me of that time, that world long ago, when I so desperately sought to bond with my largely absent father and never succeeded. It is a bittersweet memory.

It was in this environment of tranquillity, with occasional interruptions — a cat jumping across the word processor, or a dog suddenly giving a yelp to remind you that it's time to take a walk — that I could let my thoughts roam. I closed my eyes and poured out my feelings, which eventually found their way into the characters of my novels.

I was in a jubilant mood when Ushi drove me to Santa Paula Airport for my return trip to Beverly Hills. My friend Noel Blanc, son of the master of cartoon voices, Mel Blanc, and an avid helicopter

My horse, Sport, a leading character in my novel, *The Gift*. (© *Lori Hofferber*)

pilot, had offered to pick me up and ferry me back.

Waiting for Noel to arrive, Ushi and I had lunch at the airport restaurant and watched the little planes buzzing around, landing, taking off. We were watching Lee and David, but I didn't know them yet. I didn't know how important they would become to me.

Soon enough, we saw Noel's helicopter approaching. We left the restaurant, walked past the parked planes toward the runway and met Noel and his friend and copilot, Mike Carra, a Beverly Hills police officer.

"Hey, Noel," I said, "would you believe it? Ushi has never been in a helicopter."

"Well, we have the time, let's take her for a ride," Noel said.

We climbed aboard and flew low over my Garden of Eden, passing over a grove where earlier that morning I had stolen a half-dozen grapefruit that were now stashed in the cargo compartment. We zoomed over Ushi's house and frightened my horse Sport in his paddock. Sport, unbeknownst to him, was going to star in *The Gift*.

We passed a small plane in the sky practicing maneuvers. Lee and David's plane?

Finally we headed back for the airport to let Ushi out. We drifted down to the landing pad by the side of the main runway. Noel kept the blades turning, since we would be taking off for home right away.

Ushi had loved her first ride in a helicopter and yelled her thanks as Mike, the copilot, let her out. She ran across the runway and stood on the side, waving to us as we prepared to lift off.

David and Lee had just landed — Ushi noticed their little plane rolling slowly along the taxiway.

At the same time our helicopter started to rise. Looking out of the window, I admired the view, the mountain range seemingly on fire in the afternoon sun. In my headset, I could hear Noel's voice reciting the litany at takeoff. It sounded like "The fox tangos with a zebra."

We started to rise.

At that precise moment, David and Lee were taxiing down the runway, gathering speed for another touch-and-go. They lifted off the ground, starting *their* climb to the sky. We met fifty feet above the ground.

In that horrible fraction of a second, the rotating blades of Noel's Bell Ranger helicopter sliced into the wing of David and Lee's Pitts, ripping it open and exposing its fuel to air. Carried by its fateful momentum, the little plane continued to rise forward into the blue sky. An instant later, the fuel caught fire. The Pitts exploded in a fireball.

The helicopter, its rotors torn off by the impact, crashed to the tarmac.

But we were alive in the tangled wreckage. David and Lee were dead in the smoldering remains.

At that moment I was unconscious. I didn't know that I had met David and Lee. I didn't know what they would come to mean to me. I didn't know that from this day forward I would be asking: Why did they die? Why was I alive?

CHAPTER
TWO

Ushi had seen the whole thing. She had witnessed David and Lee's fiery death, and she stood frozen by the side of the runway. One of the blades ripped from the helicopter by the impact had flown toward her, crashing into and damaging a parked plane near where she was standing, but she hadn't noticed.

Wanting to help me get out of the wreckage, she ran through the falling fiery debris, not hearing someone screaming, "Get away, it's gonna blow!" She scrambled helplessly to the top of the over-turned helicopter to reach the door, the engine still running and leaking fuel. Finally, the warnings penetrated: "Get away, it's gonna blow."

The person screaming at her was a flight mechanic named Darryl who had been working in a nearby hangar. He ran toward the wreckage. Unlike Ushi, who was oblivious to the dangers, Darryl, a former medic who served in Vietnam, knew that the helicopter could blow at any moment. Yet he risked his life to save perfect strangers. Now that's a hero.

Darryl passed Mike, the copilot, who had been thrown free from the wreckage and was crawling away, and reached into the cockpit — past the bleeding and badly injured Noel — and turned off the motor.

Atop the helicopter Ushi looked down into the carcass of the passenger compartment. She could see me huddled in a heap at the bottom, one side of my face covered with blood. Her first thought was that I was dead.

Often, when I am asked about the accident today, people want to know what I experienced at that moment. Did I see a long tunnel with a blazing white light at the other end? Sorry, I saw and heard nothing. If it was there, I missed the show.

They tell me that within minutes policemen, firemen and ambulances converged, and that I was moaning, "My back, my back." Fearing a spine injury, the firemen had to strap me to a backboard before they could lift me out of the wreckage. In such a small space, they had to lower one of their buddies upside down, holding him by the legs so that he could strap me up properly.

While they were working on this awkward task, Ushi called my wife.

Anne was in her office finishing up her work. We had a dinner date with friends that night, and she still had to have her hair and nails done. The phone rang.

"Don't worry, Anne," Ushi reported breathlessly. "There was a helicopter crash, but Kirk is all right. He just has some cuts on his face and probably a couple ribs are broken."

To Ushi, what she was saying was great news. Only minutes before she thought I was dead. In comparison, a few broken ribs were nothing.

Meanwhile, Anne pictured me as a bleeding and broken mess. She was in shock but pulled herself together and called our sons Peter and Eric. She didn't want them to hear it from the news media. And, sure enough, as she was talking to the boys, TV and newspaper reporters were already calling on the other line.

Peter and Eric quickly met her at the office, where they prepared to drive up to Santa Paula, a two-hour ride. Panic-stricken, Peter called the police to ask for an escort to get there more quickly. He was told that would not help — rush hour had started, and traffic north of Los Angeles was already bumper to bumper. At the same airport where our helicopter had been scheduled to land, he got a helicopter to fly the three of them to the Santa Paula Memorial Hospital.

I have no remembrance of being pulled out of the wreckage, put in an ambulance and brought to the emergency room. I have no recollection of X rays, CAT scans and the doctors' examinations. They tell me that when the radiologist said, "We have to roll you over," I muttered, "I don't think I'm gonna like it," and the people in the emergency room laughed. But I don't remember any of that.

The first thing I do remember is looking up and seeing my wife's eyes staring at me. This was three hours later. I have no memory of the time in between, even though they tell me I was fully conscious.

The next thing I remember was that they

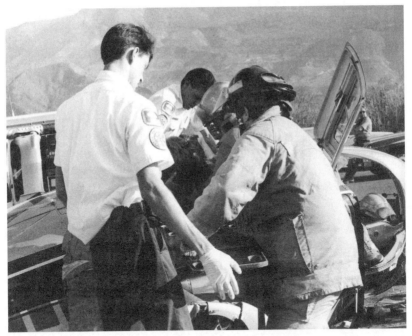

Firemen trying to get me out of the helicopter wreck. (© *Associated Press*)

They are carrying me off to the hospital.
(© *Santa Paula Chronicle/Gamma Liaison*)

wheeled me in a gurney and put me in a helicopter — just what I needed, another ride in a helicopter! But Anne wanted to move me to our hospital near Beverly Hills, Cedars-Sinai Medical Center. Anne and Eric came with me, along with a young woman doctor. I couldn't have been that bad off — I remember that she was very pretty.

I don't know how they got me into intensive care at Cedars. Vaguely, I was aware of flashbulbs going off — the media were doing their job. Then a blur of more X rays, tests, CAT scans. And finally I was left alone in my room.

Now the medication was wearing off and the pain was growing stronger. My back hurt like hell. I couldn't move in any direction. Trying to lift up my head was agonizing. I just lay there, feeling sorry for myself.

And then the young woman doctor told me off. "You are lucky, Kirk. Pain means you're not paralyzed. Be happy you can feel things." Before I could react, she added, "The people in the plane are dead."

That's how I found out that David and Lee had died. For the first time I heard their names. Somewhere out there, not too many miles from where I lay, the lives of people who loved them were forever changed . . . and now mine had as well.

CHAPTER

THREE

I was lying in bed at Cedars-Sinai; every move of my body was agony. I started to curse, but then a wave of guilt came over me. I was deeply ashamed of feeling sorry for myself when young David and his instructor Lee were dead. Dead. I was alive.

"Thank God I am alive," I said. Then I caught myself. We all say "Thank God" automatically when we have a narrow escape, but do we *mean* it? I'm not sure I did.

I hadn't thought about God for a long time. I ran away from Him many, many years ago.

You see, I got frightened at age fourteen by the story of Abraham and Isaac. God orders Abraham to go up on the mountain and sacrifice his only son, Isaac. I remember the picture in my Sunday-school book — Abraham, with a long beard, in one outstretched hand holding a large knife, in the other a frightened little boy. And that kid looked an awful lot like me. A hovering angel was having a hard time restraining Abraham. How could he convince Abraham that God was only testing him?

Wow! Some test! Some God!

That picture stayed in my mind for a long time as I drifted away from religion. I grew up, went to college, got married, but my view of God stayed stuck in a fourteen-year-old's Sunday-school book.

I have to admit that, as I lay in that hospital bed aching all over, my feelings about God had not progressed much beyond that point. That I paused to say "Thank God" was just a reflex reaction. But, of course, I was sincerely grateful to be alive. Then I thought of the families of David and Lee. If I say "Thank God," what do *they* say?

These thoughts began to bother me, but I pushed them away. I went back to feeling sorry for myself. It's humiliating to be a patient in the hospital when you are conscious and aware of everything. You just lie there with a needle stuck in your veins, and you amuse yourself by counting the drops of liquid falling into the tube. Then you have to take a piss. But the nurse won't take you to the bathroom. You tell her with a little help you can make it. Ah no, she gives you a bottle to use. They have to measure the exact amount of that precious liquid. So you lie there, helpless, as they stuff you with antibiotics and painkillers.

They are also extremely interested in bowel movements, and they inquire about that several times a day as they point to a shiny bedpan next to you. When nothing happens, the nurse declares that I am constipated from the painkillers and gives me a laxative.

Of course the magic elixir decides to work suddenly in the middle of the night. I ring for the nurse, but she doesn't come. I look over at that shiny bedpan. I just can't use this thing. I absolutely cannot do it. But I have to do something. I ring again. Nothing.

By this time nature is not to be denied. I can't figure out how to lower the bed rail, so I climb over it. In the process, I manage to rip the IV needle out of my arm. My back is killing me. I break out in a cold sweat, but I make it to the bathroom just in time.

The nurse comes in and finds me trying to crawl back to bed. She helps me, sticks the needle back in and reprimands me like a little child. My back is aching, but I feel triumphant because the bedpan is still shiny.

Finally, I convinced my doctor that I could do just as well squawking about my aches and pains at home. I am sure my nurses were glad to get rid of me.

At last I was in my own bedroom, which is also my study. This is my favorite place, where I work on my scripts and my books. It's a haven where I can stretch out on my daybed and dream.

I had a lot of time for that, waiting for the pain to leave me. I would lean back on my pillow and look up at the Chagall lithographs that hang on the wall alongside my bed. It's a collection of his Bible series that I bought some time ago because I liked the colors and his simple, almost naive, style.

I had looked at them often, but now, for the first time, I actually *saw* their faces — Abraham, Moses, David. All those old patriarchs seemed to be telling me something, although I wasn't sure what their message was. Maybe, I thought, I could find some answers in the Bible, but I didn't think that I could even find a Bible in my library.

I tried other ways of coping with my guilt — "survivor's guilt," they call it. I saw a psychiatrist. Then another.

One of them said to me, "Kirk, it seems that you are preoccupied with death."

"What do you mean?" I asked in irritation.

"You seem to be preparing yourself for death," he said, sounding like an oracle.

"Well, isn't all of life a preparation for death?" I retorted, trying to sound like an even greater oracle.

I can't remember his response because suddenly I thought of something I had written about sixty years before as a teenage poet: "Life is a lock and death the only key." I didn't dare quote those lines to him, because I wasn't sure I knew what the hell I was writing then . . . or now, for that matter. But I suspect that on some primitive level I felt, more than understood, what Albert Schweitzer meant when he wrote: "Thinking about death . . . produces true love for life. When we are familiar with death, we accept each week, each day, as a gift."

I wondered if David and Lee had done anything to help prepare themselves for death. David's uncle had died in a plane crash, and Lee's second wife was the widow of a pilot who had died in a crash at the same airport, so they knew the dangers of flying. But they were young, with so much of life ahead of them. How could they take the possibility of their own death even halfway seriously?

I began to ask questions about them, collected

clippings. I learned about who they were. They became real to me — not strangers, not just some faceless victims of an accident.

But still, the thought was ever-present in my mind: *They* were dead. I was alive.

Why do some people live and others die?

I lay there and I thought about other times when I could have died.

I was ten years old when they began construction on a mill next to our house. To lay the foundation, they dug a trench, five feet deep, which filled with water from a broken pipe. While playing there, I placed a narrow board over the water in the trench and tried to walk across. But I slipped and fell in. I couldn't swim. I still vividly remember bobbing up and down in the water. I could see my two frightened playmates running away. But Wolfie, one of the older boys, stayed behind and pulled me out. He couldn't swim either. Why did he do it?

I lay there absorbing the impact of that early memory when the second one came into focus. The year was 1955, I was thirty-eight, shooting *The Indian Fighter* in Oregon. We were doing a scene where I was standing up in the ramparts of a wooden fort, shooting a rifle through the notched beams, while the stuntmen who were playing the Indians shot arrows with four-inch steel heads at the fort. Those things were sharp! The cameras rolled while I stood on a ledge, peering through slits between logs, firing my rifle. Suddenly, a flaming arrow dug into the beam about six inches from my head. I felt weak all over. That had not been planned. If that arrow had been just six inches closer, it could have ended my life.

My thoughts turned to a day in Palm Springs when I was forty-one years old. Mike Todd, a colorful producer who was living around the corner from us with his new wife, Elizabeth Taylor, invited me to fly to New York with him in his private plane. He was to receive an award there, but Elizabeth had a terrible cold and couldn't fly. En route we would stop in Missouri and visit President Truman, a pal of Mike's. The trip sounded like fun, and I agreed to leave with him the next day. But my wife Anne was against it. She hated the idea of me flying in a small private plane. We had a bitter argument. "Why don't you take a commercial flight and meet him there?" she asked. I tried to explain that the fun of the trip would be flying with Mike. The argument became more intense; in the end, I didn't go. Anne and I weren't speaking with each other the next morning as we drove back to Beverly Hills. I turned on the radio and listened to Mozart as we silently sped down the freeway. The music was interrupted by a bulletin — Mike Todd's plane had gone down in a storm; Mike and everyone on board had been killed. I pulled over to the side of the highway and looked at Anne.

Why wasn't I on that plane?

Next my thoughts turned to Spain. I was shooting a movie with Yul Brynner, *The Light at the Edge of the World*. It was 1970 and I was fifty-three, still a young man. I was staying in Cadaqués, next door to Salvador Dalí. The day he came to watch the shooting, we were doing a scene in the woods. We had constructed a hut on rocky terrain. The scene called for me to be on the roof of this hut when I get shot. I was then to roll off the roof onto the rocks below, or so it would appear on film. Of course, a mattress was placed on a scaffold constructed just below the roof and out of view of the camera. For further insurance a stuntman was standing there to break my fall.

I rolled off the roof too fast, the stuntman couldn't stop me, and I fell on the rocks below. I suffered a concussion, but, like so many people in shock from an injury, I didn't even know it — I didn't feel any pain. I insisted they wipe the blood off my head; then I climbed on the roof again and did another take. After that, I passed out and was taken to the hospital, where I didn't regain consciousness for several days. Again I was lucky. Many people under the same circumstances don't ever come out of a coma, but I did, complaining that I was hungry.

After the helicopter crash, I was told that a significant amount of scar tissue from that concussion appeared on-screen in the CAT scans.

Now, in bed, recovering again from another terrible accident, I asked, How many chances does a man get?

When you become a movie star, you create an image for the public. They begin to believe it, and you start buying into that fiction yourself. In some ways, I had come to believe that I was one of the tough guys I played. I should have paid more attention to how often my characters died on the screen!

Tough Guys was the title of the last movie I made with Burt Lancaster.

Poor Burt. A year before my accident he had suffered a stroke, and his right side was completely paralyzed. He could make guttural sounds, but he couldn't speak. He spent his days in bed or in a wheelchair. I thought a lot about him as I lay in bed. Was this the end of the tough guys? In one way or the other, it was the end. Because certainly we would never be so tough again.

CHAPTER

FOUR

Two weeks after being released from the hospital, I had to put my aches and pains aside and go out into the public spotlight. The occasion, months in the planning, was the banquet for the American Film Institute Lifetime Achievement Award, of which I was the 1991 recipient.

It was a prestigious award — only one was given each year — and I was proud to be chosen to join the ranks of James Cagney, Orson Welles, Alfred Hitchcock, Fred Astaire and other greats.

But I was in bad shape. My back was still black and blue, and so was my face. For the event, a make-up man had skillfully covered my black eye. Stiffly I entered the ballroom to be greeted by loud applause and a sea of smiling faces. It felt good. The most difficult part of that evening was having to endure the congratulatory slaps on the back. Every slap sent jabs of pain through my body.

I tried to sit erect throughout the ceremony. I was genuinely touched by the many complimentary things that were said by stars such as Tom Cruise, Sylvester Stallone, Richard Harris, Danny De Vito, Dana Carvey, Lauren Bacall, Jean Simmons, even my son Michael. But what meant the most to me was that my grandson Cameron, an avid baseball player, had given up his practice to see the old man receive an honor that had nothing to do with baseball.

It was a great evening, but I was happy when it was all over. With Anne, I wended my way through the crowd, carrying the heavy silver star they gave me. I was exhausted, and in pain, and really didn't feel like smiling, but I did — a modest, friendly smile, I hoped. All I could think about was returning to bed. My back was killing me.

The next day it still hurt, and the next week, and the next month. No matter how carefully I followed doctor's orders, no matter how much I pampered myself, the pain would not go away.

After more tests, I was told that the impact of the crash had compressed my spine, and I was shocked to learn that I had lost almost three inches in height. The compression aggravated old injuries and spurred into action nerve endings that had nothing to do before. One nerve tract — the sciatic — travels from the spine through the hip to the knees, and it can cause trouble in any number of spots. My back ached, my hip was immobilized and my knees felt like old doors with rusty hinges.

Many doctors examined me. I had more film of me in X rays than I had in movies. Dr. Ted Goldstein shook his head when he looked over the X rays. "You did most of your own stunts in movies, huh?"

"Yes, I did."

"I can see them."

"So fix me up."

He laughed. "I'll give you some anti-inflammatory drugs, because I don't want to operate on you — I wouldn't know where to begin."

He recommended I cut down on activities if I wanted to feel less pain — say, nine holes of golf instead of eighteen. I was angry. This was the best modern medicine could offer — "Don't know where to begin ... anti-inflammatories ... cut down on golf"?

Friends recommended I try some alternative treatments. I heard about a doctor in Santa Monica who was supposedly responsible for phenomenal cures with acupuncture and herbs. While the thought of needles being stuck into my body didn't exactly thrill me, the prospect of being constantly immobilized by pain was far worse, so I made an appointment.

My initial visit didn't exactly inspire confidence. Or maybe it was just me.

Things didn't go badly at first. The Chinese doctor appeared appropriately stoic, and his hands were steady. The needles were frighteningly long, but they were also very thin, as thin as hairs — you could hardly feel them being stuck into your body.

The thing about acupuncture, if you haven't had it, is that they put those things in and then they leave you alone for a half-hour while the needles work their miracle cure. You have become a human pincushion. You are sternly instructed not to move; don't even think about getting up.

I was happy enough, lying on my stomach, starting to doze, when the bed started to shake. It took me a second to figure out that I was in the middle of another Los Angeles earthquake. As a fifty-year resident of this Jell-O bowl, I am not bothered by a small earthquake. But this situation was unusual.

What should I do? Get up, go for cover? But what of the needles in my back — would they break?

Fortunately, the temblor lasted only a few seconds.

Acting as if nothing had happened, the Chinese doctor came in, took out my needles and sent me home. On my way out he handed me a plastic bag containing herbs that he said must be cooked following directions and then drunk as tea three times a day. Skeptical, I took the bag home.

When I looked inside, the so-called herbs startled me. The mixture looked like scrapings from the forest floor — pieces of bark, leaves, eyes of newt, stuff like that.

You had to boil the mess a long time, and it made the house stink. Strained, as per directions, the "tea" tasted the way it looked — like boiled dirt.

Although I went back a couple of times, I didn't notice any miraculous results. I guess you have to be a believer. So I gave it up.

I went back to maintaining the most comfortable position I could find — lying stretched out on my back in front of the TV. From that vantage point, I watched others play golf or baseball or football. But there comes a time when even an avid sports fan OD's on TV. When that happened, I would turn off the tube and just stare at my Chagall prints.

Chagall is an artist I identify with. I like his childlike style, his floating figures. The other parts of the house are filled with other painters, all of them fine. But Chagall is something special.

I met him years ago in the south of France at the Hôtel du Cap. I'll never forget those blazing blue eyes darting in every direction, like those of a curious child. My wife brought him a page from an art book with one of his small paintings reproduced in the center of the page. She asked him to autograph it for me. He smiled and took it home with him. The next day he gave it to me; he had extended the painting in the center to fill out the entire page, creating a new original, and he dedicated it to me. I was delighted. It now hangs in my room.

He invited Anne and me to his home not too far away, and he guided us around, pointing out his paintings on the walls. We stopped in front of one depicting a large, buxom woman who dwarfed a little man standing next to her.

I pointed to the woman. "Who is that?"

"My mother," he answered with extreme pride.

"And who is the little man?"

"My father," he answered, almost contemptuously.

I was surprised to learn that Chagall came from Vitebsk, a town in the Pale of Settlement where Jews were confined in White Russia, not far from Mogilev, the town my father came from. And guess what? Chagall and my father left Russia the same year, 1910. Chagall went to Paris and became a world-famous artist, and my father came to this

country and became a ragman. Jews have diverse talents.

Of course, when I was growing up in upstate New York, I rarely asked my father or my mother about their backgrounds, about Mogilev, about the people they left behind, about my relatives, about my grandparents. As a matter of fact, I can't remember hearing more from my father than, "Come here . . . go there . . . take this . . . pick up that . . ."

You don't learn much from that.

When I was a kid in school, I remember the beginning of a song we sang in the first grade: "Over the river and through the wood, to grandfather's house we'll go . . ." The songbook had a drawing of a beautiful, spirited horse prancing through the snow pulling a sleigh filled with happy children with rosy cheeks and sparkling eyes. They seemed ecstatic to be heading to their grandfather's, whom I envisioned as a jolly old man, not unlike Santa Claus, with goodies for all of them. How I envied those kids. I had no grandfather — or a grandmother either.

I knew nothing about them. All I had were my mother's vague stories of drunken cossacks racing through the town on horseback, hitting the heads of old Jews not spry enough to get out of the way. From these stories I got the idea that the birthplace of my parents was a little shtetl covered with ice and snow.

Later, from the Chagall paintings of his Russian period, I would learn just how it looked. I could stare at them and make them come to life, remem-

bering my mother's tales. My father came to the town to marry my mother and impressed the people with his strength. He took a large tub of water normally carried by two men and brought it to the house single-handed. That scene was imprinted on my mind. I could see the townspeople gaping in awe at Pa's prodigious strength, but where were Grandma and Grandpa?

Where were my ancestors? Ma and Pa were like Adam and Eve — no one came before them.

So I struggled through life with no heritage.

When I traveled to Moscow as an American movie star I tried to find the places where my parents were born. I knew the name of the place in Russian was Mogilevska Guberny. When I asked the Soviet officials about it, they burst out laughing. It seems that Russian comedians use Mogilev the way comedians here use Podunk or Paducah — to refer to a place where the hicks come from. Its citizens don't have the reputation for being very smart, because during the great migration at the turn of the century, half of them left to make a better life — in Siberia. Thank God my father wasn't among that bunch.

Of course, by the time I went looking, the Jewish settlements near Mogilev were long gone — the Nazis made sure of that — so my ancestors seemed like wisps of fog in a dim past.

I was glad when Michael's son Cameron was born. *He* at least would have grandparents.

And yet, I was damned if I was going to be called Grandpa! That was the name for some old geezer.

And so, from an early age I taught Cameron to call me Pappy. It doesn't connote age the way "Grandpa" does. In fact, you're not quite sure what it means.

When Cameron was five years old, someone asked him, "Isn't Kirk Douglas your grandfather?" and he answered, "Yes, but his real name is Pappy." Good boy, Cameron.

You must understand, I always wanted ancestors, but I didn't want to become one!

Then Michael — maybe because he was now a father and aware of a sense of family — started asking me questions about my ancestors. I was embarrassed; I had no answers.

There is nothing like pain and confinement in bed to summon melancholy thoughts. Who were my ancestors? Where had I come from? Michael's questions haunted me.

And then, like a sign from heaven, the early-morning sun hit the Chagall Bible prints on my wall. For a while, I watched the dust particles dancing along the beam of light reflected off the glass panes of the framed prints, and then I saw them. I mean I had looked at them many times before, but this was the first time I *saw* them. I recognized them.

My God, *here* were my ancestors! They go back for thousands of years and are more famous than movie stars. Chagall had caught them perfectly: Abraham giving his blessing to Isaac. Rebecca, with her favorite, Jacob. Moses, suffused in golden light, holding the tablets of the great commandments on

A few of Chagall's Bible series that hang over my bed. *(© 1997 Artists Rights Society [ARS], New York/ADAGP, Paris)*

Mount Sinai. Solomon, the wisest man on earth. Rachel, Ruth, Esther. David — who slew Goliath — playing his harp. There were musicians in my family, warriors, poets, lawgivers.

I was up to my ass in ancestors!

CHAPTER

FIVE

I have all these ancestors because I am a Jew. A Jew! A role often uncomfortable for me to play.

When I was a junior in college I had a friend, Fred Parrott, a graduate student. Fred was far from a handsome type, with a skinny frame and buck teeth. We were a strange combination, Izzy Demsky (that was what my parents changed Issur Danielovitch to in order to make it sound more American), undefeated collegiate wrestling champion, and this undernourished gentile weakling. One afternoon, as we were engaged in one of our typical discussions on life, he stopped and looked at me strangely. He shook his head and said with a tone of great pity, "How awful it must be to be a Jew."

My immediate response was to laugh. It wasn't so bad. I was getting good grades in school, I was president of the student body, I had a beautiful girlfriend. Poor Fred had made no particular mark of distinction on anything, and he had trouble getting a date.

But later, in my room, alone with my thoughts, I agreed — it was awful being a Jew.

I remembered as a little boy running home crying to my mother, blood running from my nose: "Ma, Ma . . . big Johnny beat me up. Why does he hate me? He said I killed Jesus. I didn't kill him. I didn't. I don't even know who he is."

I remembered trying to get a job delivering the local paper, the *Amsterdam Evening Recorder.* It was an easy job — every home in the richer section got the paper. You just went down the streets throwing a paper at every door. Two blocks, and you were through. But I couldn't get that job. They didn't want Jew boys delivering their paper. Why did they hate me?

At that time there was no use trying to get a job in the carpet mills, the industry that dominated the town. They didn't take Jews either.

Going to Hebrew school each day after attending regular school was a dangerous adventure. Running home, I had to evade the gangs on the corners of East Main Street, lurking to beat me up.

My first month in college, I remember being invited to have dinner at the Alpha Tau Omega fraternity house, a prelude to becoming a member. I was excited. I got scrubbed up, borrowed a jacket and tie, and waited in the downstairs office as the other kids went down to the cafeteria for dinner. Everything quieted down, and I waited. The kids were coming back from dinner, and I waited. Nobody came, nobody called. The next day I learned that they had thought that the Demsky boy was Polish. When they found out I was a Jew they didn't want me.

Of course, when I became a star on the wrestling team and the president of the student body, they were willing to make an exception. They would give me "house privileges." This meant that I could pay rent and live at the fraternity house, but I would not be allowed to attend the brotherhood meetings or, heaven forbid, exchange the secret handshake. I despised all that bullshit, and, of course, didn't join. But, you know, it hurt. All those episodes hurt. I was the little kid who gets hit with a rock and says, "Ha, ha — it didn't hurt." But it did.

Sometimes people thought they were paying me a compliment when they said, "You don't *look* Jewish." I didn't take it as such, but I do remember once telling somebody that I was only half-Jewish. Did I think that would cut the hurt in half?

When I left college for New York to seek my fortune, I legally changed my name to Kirk Douglas. Did I really change it because I thought that Issur Danielovitch wouldn't look good on a marquee (unless I became a ballet dancer)? Or did I hope that the change would make me more acceptable? I don't know, but I do know that the name Kirk Douglas proved a mixed blessing.

I will never forget my invitation to become a member of the Westside Tennis Club when I first got noticed in Hollywood. Lex Barker, better known as Tarzan, showed me the facilities and then whispered confidentially, "Of course, Kirk, you understand, we can't run a club the way we do back East. Here we have to let in a few Jews." When I retorted, "I am a Jew," he became flustered. He wasn't a bad guy; that was just the way it was. Or is it still that way?

I think back. Why did I say to Lex Barker, "I am a Jew"? I was born that way, sure, but I now had a

41

nice Scottish name, and people said I looked like a Norwegian. (In fact, when I tried to get a job in the Yiddish theater in New York, they told me, "If we have a part for a Nazi, we'll call you.") I was circumcised, of course, but, in America, most men are. I didn't observe any Jewish religious practices, except for fasting on Yom Kippur. (In *The Bad and the Beautiful* it was difficult making love to Lana Turner on an empty stomach; of course, nobody knew it.) So why did I have to admit it?

As I look back on my life, I realize that I often express my deepest feelings through make-believe, through a role that I play in a movie or on the stage. It's as if I face myself only obliquely.

My first attempt, back in 1980, at expressing myself more directly — through a character of *my own* creation — was in a novel.

I started to write a story about a little Jewish boy named Moishe. He and his sister Rachel are inmates in a concentration camp. Like so many Jews — like Kafka — he asks, What crime have we committed? Why are we here?

Rachel's voice was hardly above a whisper: "We're here because we're Jews."

For a long time nothing was said, and then Moishe broke the silence. "Let's not be Jews."

"What are you talking about?"

"You just said it — we're here because we are Jews. So let's not be Jews."

"We were born Jews — you were named after

Moses, our great leader. We will always be Jews. Now go to sleep."

Moishe pulled the covers tightly around him. He looked up into the darkness and thought, I don't want to be a Jew. He hoped that Rachel wouldn't hear his thoughts.

As I read those lines that I had written years ago, I wondered how much of it was what I personally felt. I don't know.

I toyed with publishing the novel, but in the end I put it away in a drawer, unfinished. I didn't know at the time that before I could complete that novel I had a more basic kind of examination to go through. Before I could start writing novels, I had to write my autobiography.

One day I was playing golf at the Tamarisk Country Club in Palm Springs, a haven for retired Jews. A group of elderly gentlemen arrived on the first tee at the same time as our foursome. I said to one of our partners, "Let those old geezers tee off first."

My friend bent his head toward my ear and whispered, "Kirk, those old geezers are twelve to fifteen years younger than you."

This startled me. I studied these "old geezers" as they moved ahead of us. Balding. Some with pot bellies. Bent over. They were much younger than I was? Where have all the years gone? I asked myself. Who pressed the fast-forward button?

I don't know what my score was on that round of

golf. I was bewildered. Wasn't it only a few years ago that I took that train ride from Broadway to Hollywood? How long ago was it that I came here to Palm Springs for my first visit to The Racquet Club, the weekend mecca for Hollywood?

I remember it vividly. I sat in a lounge chair under a palm tree in awe as I watched Spencer Tracy hunched over a nearby table animatedly talking to a beautiful woman. Edward G. Robinson was standing by the pool puffing a cigar. Errol Flynn! I couldn't believe it! He sauntered in, teeth gleaming, skin bronzed, muscled like a Greek god, a tennis racket in one arm and a stunning nymphet clinging to the other.

What was I doing in this hallowed group? The year was 1946, and I had just started my first movie, *The Strange Love of Martha Ivers*, working with Barbara Stanwyck and Van Heflin. It was Heflin who got me in here.

For so many years I was "the young newcomer." Even when I saw my name above the title, inside I still felt that I hadn't arrived yet. Like Midge Kelly in *Champion*, I was still punching my way to the top. "Those fat bellies with the big cigars ain't gonna make a monkey out of me . . . I'm not gonna be a hey-you all my life. I wanna hear people call me Mister." Even when people did call me Mister, I didn't hear it. I didn't feel it inside.

It was all make-believe. One picture after another. Three pictures a year. Four pictures a year. Producing, acting, even directing. I was on fast forward.

I was shocked when someone first called me "a

veteran." By that time I had made several dozen movies. When was I first jolted by someone calling me "a legend"? What happened?

One day I was driving to Palm Springs when I saw a young sailor hitchhiking. This brought back memories of my time in the Navy, and I stopped the car to give him a lift. The young fellow jumped in. "Gee, thanks a lot —" and then gave a double take. "Are you . . . you . . ." he stammered, and finally got it out. "Do you know who you are?"

A good question. Who *was* I?

I began to struggle with that question when, in 1985, I started to write my life story, *The Ragman's Son*. Did I tell all? Sorry, no. But I tried to be honest. It was important to me to examine my life — to try to make sense of my public image and the real inner me that is frightened, vulnerable, threatened and a lot softer than the exterior man.

I remember that one of the things that was the most difficult to include in that book was a chapter I wrote about my pacemaker. Admitting that my heart does not always function well on its own and needs mechanical help made me feel very vulnerable. But somehow it poured out of me — I wrote that whole chapter, which I called "Music Box," in one evening. Then I got cold feet. Why tell the world something so personal? I didn't have to tell all. There were other things that were too deeply personal to include. Maybe this too should be kept private, I said to myself. But would the book be honest without it? So it may destroy a few illusions that the great tough guy, the great gunfighter, the great champion boxer, has a hunk of metal in his chest — so be it. Also, it might help an awful lot of people understand what it means to have a pacemaker. Finally, I did put that chapter in the book.

Who am I? Among other things, I am a man with a pacemaker.

Other questions followed: Where did I come from? Where am I going?

Where did I come from? That was easy. But where am I going? That was something else.

CHAPTER
SIX

It was difficult for me to ask myself: *Where are you going?*

The question irritated me. It was one of those "big" questions that come in a package along with: *What is the meaning of life? Why are we here? Who is God?*

I'd much rather run away and drown myself in work, make a movie, silence the questions of reality in the world of make-believe. So, when my son Peter came to me in the fall of 1987 with a script for a remake of *Inherit the Wind* — the story of the creation-versus-evolution debate between Clarence Darrow and William Jennings Bryan — I jumped at the chance to escape once again.

And yet, the script's subject matter, oddly enough, was steering me toward the answer to the very question that I was trying to avoid. But I didn't see it then. I just thought it would be challenging to play Bryan, the defender of the literal belief in the biblical account of creation.

I didn't know it at the time but, had Bryan been Jewish, he wouldn't have made a fool of himself in that courtroom, because the Jewish reading of the Bible is quite compatible with evolution. It simply holds that in whatever manner human beings

A scene with Jason Robards and Jean Simmons from *Inherit the Wind*. Jason won an Emmy. As usual, I was a loser — too much chin.
(© *Vincent Pictures*)
My son Peter produced *Inherit the Wind* and won an Emmy, too.

evolved there was a point when the ape-man got a soul, and that guy was Adam. Darrow would have had nothing to argue with.

For the part of Darrow, I tried to get Gregory Peck. Greg and I had never worked together, but I always admired him as a person — and an actor. We started out together on the New York stage about the same time, but he became a leading man immediately, working opposite the legendary Katharine Cornell, while I was ecstatic to get a bit part as a Western Union messenger singing four lines to the tune of "Yankee Doodle Dandy."

We had several talks about *Inherit the Wind*. And had an immediate difference of opinion. When I discuss a script I tend to become animated. On the other hand Greg is just the opposite — very quiet, very polite, but very firm. What is more, Greg is a purist, and he wanted to stick to the original version. I, on the other hand, saw no point in trying to make the same movie again, already a classic with Spencer Tracy; I wanted a different take on the old story. We couldn't come to an agreement, and Jason Robards ended up playing the part.

He was brilliant. He won an Emmy for his performance. My son Peter won an Emmy as executive producer. My record was intact — still a loser.

While I was filming *Inherit the Wind*, the manuscript of my autobiography was at Simon & Schuster being edited by Michael Korda. I admired Michael a lot and enjoyed his books; in fact, I played a part in the miniseries based on his bestselling novel, *Queenie*. But we had one major disagreement regarding my book.

I felt I couldn't tell the story of Kirk Douglas and ignore the real me, Issur, the little boy inside of my belly. (This was before all those books like *Iron John* came out dealing with the child within.) I couldn't tell people that macho man Kirk Douglas was scared or embarrassed; macho man Kirk Douglas yelled and cursed and stormed out of the room. It was little Issur who hurt in silence and closed the door so that he could nurse his wounds alone. Issur was the vulnerable part of me. I could not tell my story without including Issur; but Michael Korda disagreed.

So we had a problem. How could I ignore Issur? While Kirk was carousing with the stars, Issur had been so lonely. He had been lonely all his life, the only boy in a family of six sisters. Oh, how Issur longed for his father, who was rarely there.

For a while, Issur slept with his sisters, sharing a bed with the oldest, Betty. He liked that. She would read to him every night. Then he was shunted to a hard couch in the parlor — alone. Ruth, Fritzie and Ida were in one bed, Kay, Marion and Betty in another. Pa — when he came home late at night — slept with Ma. Only Issur was alone.

And yet, at other times, Issur sought solitude, trying to escape the tumult of that small house, the yakking of his six sisters. He would go to a field at the edge of town and lie down in the tall weeds beside a pond and look up at the sky. Was God really up there above these puffy clouds? he would wonder.

In college, Issur, who was by then buried deep within me, dictated that I should be alone most of the time. I didn't like having a roommate. I now wanted to sleep alone. Was it the habit of that hard couch in the parlor? During World War II, when I was in midshipman school at Notre Dame, I hated sleeping four people in a room; aboard ship I didn't like sharing space with even one other officer.

The pattern of my life kept me apart from others. When I came to Hollywood, every major actor was signed to a studio; I was a maverick and worked alone. I envied the other guys going to speech and dancing classes with pretty girls. I was still Issur with his nose pressed up against a pastry-store window.

Forming my own production company made me even more lonely. I was the boss, but who likes the boss? Certainly, directors and writers and other actors don't like working for an actor. My life in Hollywood was spent preparing and making movies — three, sometimes four, a year. In this world of make-believe, fantasies and dreams, I didn't have to deal with Issur, the little Jewish boy who never really belonged. I preferred to deal with the people of my dreams. Trust me — you meet a better class of people in your dreams.

In this hectic world I didn't take the time to get in touch with myself. It wasn't until the movies stopped coming one after another; it wasn't until I hit my sixties that I began consciously thinking about Issur and how, in many ways, he inwardly dictated the life of Kirk Douglas. Finally, in my auto-

51

biography, I had confessed to the world that I was Issur. Finally, I had given him a voice. This was a voice that Michael Korda wanted to silence. He wanted to erase Issur.

Although I fought to save Issur, Michael Korda was insistent, and he was the editor-in-chief of Simon & Schuster. Perhaps he was right when he said that the device was too sentimental. Perhaps people only wanted the kiss-and-tell stuff. Figuring he should know what makes a book sell, I reluctantly acquiesced in his suggestions and started murdering little Issur.

But seeing my unhappiness, Korda decided to get a second opinion. He sent the manuscript to Ushi, who was working under contract for Simon & Schuster.

Fortunately for me, Ushi disagreed with her boss. She felt that the Issur passages gave the book depth. In fact, she thought there should be *more* of Issur, not less. She convinced Michael Korda, and Issur was resurrected. I insisted on meeting her to thank her personally. It didn't occur to me till later that Ushi had saved the Jewish part of me — Issur was my Hebrew name, a nickname for Israel.

In September of 1988 *The Ragman's Son* finally arrived in bookstores. The first week it was number nine on *The New York Times* bestseller list, and I complained. The next week it was number two — and I still wasn't happy.

My friend Sidney Sheldon said, "Kirk, you are

crazy. The first time a book of mine made the best-seller list, I cried with happiness. Look at the great reviews you got from *The New York Times* . . . the *Washington Post*." He shook his head in disgust.

But I had never been able to interpret reviews. I remember an early one in *The New York Times* for the play *The Wind Is Ninety*: "Kirk Douglas is nothing short of superb." That night I lay in bed next to my first wife, Diana, muttering to myself, "Nothing, nothing . . . why nothing?" I jabbed Diana in the ribs. "Why couldn't they just say, 'Kirk Douglas is superb'?"

Still, the success of my book shocked me. I believe that failure is much easier to handle than success — failure is something that we have in common with so many other people. Success makes you stand out, it makes you a target. You become vulnerable.

All my life I sought a pat on the back, the approval of applause. That's probably one of the reasons I became an actor. And I never got enough. It took me a long time to learn that my desire for approval was insatiable, that it could never be fulfilled. My satisfaction had to come from the doing. When a project was done, on to the next one.

It is difficult for me to look back. That's why in my home I have no awards, posters or mementos of what I've done. My excitement is derived from looking ahead. I always lived by the the lines of Alfred, Lord Tennyson:

How dull it is to pause, to make an end,
To rust unburnished, not to shine in use . . .

So, I forgot about being number two on the best-seller list; in fact, I *did* get to be number one on the paperback list, but by then I didn't care. In the meantime, I had pulled out of the drawer the novel I had written so many years before. Of course, it needed a lot of work. I asked Ushi if it was worth it. She said yes. I went to work, and soon my agent had made a deal with Random House to publish it under the title *Dance with the Devil*.

I was more amazed than anyone — but very pleased — to have this new "career." I liked the role of being a writer. I thought of buying a pipe, even though I had given up smoking years before. It seemed to go with the role. I would try to speak more slowly and become more pensive. I would put movies behind me. I had made enough of them — almost eighty. That part of my career was over, I thought. Ideas for my second novel were already bouncing around in my head.

But then temptation came calling . . .

CHAPTER

SEVEN

Temptation came calling in the person of a charming French director with impeccable credentials. When, in the fall of 1990, he approached me to make a movie in the French language as well as in English, I was listening.

See, even though I proclaimed loudly that my creative needs were more adequately satisfied by writing and that I had no intention of making more movies, all the while — in the back of my mind — I was a little afraid that, at my age, I wouldn't be offered any more movie roles.

Now here was an offer I couldn't refuse. I would act in two languages — what a temptation to the ego. I could see it so clearly. A big close-up of me on the screen speaking French. Another big close-up speaking English. In France they would say, *"Merveilleux"*; here, "Superb."

Of course I can say anything I want about this movie now, because none of you have ever seen it.

Geaarard Depardieu was going to play a smaller part. That intrigued me. But when Depardieu fell out, that should have told me something. I had second thoughts about doing the movie, but how could I abandon this intelligent director who was so impressed with my linguistic abilities, who was so willing to make every change in the script that I requested?

Besides, he was just overjoyed with my "brilliant" idea of utilizing clips from a movie that I made in French more than forty years ago, *Act of Love*, which featured the young Brigitte Bardot in a bit part. My ego was running amok.

I did make the movie. I made it in both languages and it was a flop — in both languages. But I am not altogether sorry, because it did give me a chance to spend a month in the breathtaking landscape of the French Pyrenees.

And it gave me the opportunity to visit Lourdes. This is a place where people who are in search of God go. There can't be another place like it on earth. Let me put it another way — I hope there isn't.

To appreciate the "uniqueness" of Lourdes you have to picture the Pyrenees. Majestic mountains, dense prehistoric forests, bucolic pastures. Little villages straight from the seventeenth century. Stone houses, thatch-roofed barns. Narrow country roads empty of traffic, often blocked by herds of sheep or goats moving from pasture to barn. Peasants driving rickety wagons. A place where time stood still.

And then you come to Lourdes. The huge billboards approaching the town give you a clue that something is going to be different here. Sure enough, it is. Very soon you are in bumper-to-bumper traffic, making your way down a gauntlet of nothing but souvenir shops. On both sides of the road. For a solid mile.

You can get the Holy Mary or St. Bernadette

A moment in *Veraz*, the movie you never saw. A lot of acting went to waste — from me, not the bear.
(© *M. Pelletier/Sygma*)

made out of every imaginable substance. You want her out of soap? You got her. Want her on your watch? How about a clear plastic bottle in the shape of the Holy Mary with a blue screw-cap crown? That's for the holy water that heals the sick.

I had seen nothing like it. But since then I've learned that the "holy" vulgarity that had shocked me in Lourdes is worse in the United States. Here it's a three-billion-dollar business.

According to a September 24, 1995, article in the *Los Angeles Times* reporting on a recent religious convention, "If Jesus had been in Denver this summer he could have thumbed through the pages of a bulletproof New Testament, posed for snapshots with a superhero named Bibleman, or shopped for a Last Supper paint-by-numbers kit. Wandering the floor of the Colorado Convention Center, he would have been able to buy a Christian boomerang ('love always returns'), chomp a Scripture fortune cookie, and sniff a balm called 'Fragrance of Jesus.'"

All this without the benefit of a miracle site like Lourdes, where a little girl named Bernadette had a vision in a meadow while tending sheep.

The meadow is now cemented over and lined on all sides by countless water faucets from which you can get the aforementioned holy water. They've dammed up the stream and pressurized the flow for the convenience of the faithful.

There is a huge church, of course, and a re-created scene of the grotto where it happened. The babbling brook is protected by a plastic shield in the shape of a toilet-seat cover. I kid you not.

The crippled, the lame, those riddled with cancer, line up hoping that they will be healed if they only touch this spot where a little peasant girl said she had seen the Holy Mary.

But perhaps that little girl stayed out later than she should have that night. Perhaps she had been with the farmer's son and needed an excuse when she came home. Suddenly, she had a divine inspiration: "Ma, Pa, you'll never believe it — a miracle!"

You are probably saying, "Kirk, why are you so cynical? If you don't believe in this, what *do* you believe in?"

You know what? I am not that cynical. I'm quite willing to believe that a sweet, innocent girl did have a vision. Children have an openness that allows them to connect with the spiritual world. They haven't yet erected the barriers of "knowledge" that seem to bar adult communication with God.

But if these people believe, then how — in good conscience — can they put that little girl's sacred experience on a key chain or a T-shirt? And what of those sick souls who go there wanting a shortcut to God, a quick fix for their suffering? Do they think that God is there beneath the concrete? Are they full of faith or full of doubt? Why do they travel so far to touch God? Why can't they touch God within themselves — wherever they are?

Of course, you don't have to convince me that it's really hard to connect with God on a purely spiritual level. We all would prefer a God we can see, touch, put in our back pocket — on a key chain. Didn't the Jews have the same problem three thousand years ago in the Sinai Desert? They couldn't wait forty days for Moses to descend from the mountain with the Ten Commandments. They grew impatient. So they manufactured the Golden Calf. If it were today they'd be hammering out Golden Calf key chains.

I don't mean to be a smartass. I believe in miracles. Maybe, who knows, maybe if you believe strongly enough, a miracle can happen in answer to one's prayer. Every week on TV, you see masses of people, arms upraised — many of them, like those at Lourdes, hoping for a miracle cure — as they repeat after an impassioned preacher, "I believe! I believe! I believe!"

But can blind faith alone save you?

No! What you do with your life has got to count for more than what you believe. I think what you do with that handicap, that illness, that challenge in your life, is what God pays attention to, not how loudly you pray for a cure.

Judaism holds that faith means *bubkes* if you cheat your neighbor, hit your wife or ignore the beggar on the street. It maintains that you don't have to be of a member of any particular religion to get to God, but you have to be a good person. Like Jesus said — quoting the Torah that predated him by more than a thousand years — "Love thy neighbor as thyself."

The visit to Lourdes didn't help me answer the question *Where am I going?* It didn't shed any light on *Who is God?* But it did crystallize some ideas I had for my second novel — what came to be called *The Gift* — the hero of which is a man with one leg.

60

I've always been fascinated with how handicapped people cope with life. Little did I know that I was collecting information that I would eventually need myself.

In doing research for the book, in trying to get into the skin of a handicapped person, I met an amazing young man named Jim MacLaren.

We were introduced through Dr. Albert Rappoport, a prosthetist who was fitting him for a new left leg. He had broken his old prosthesis during the running of a marathon. A one-legged man running a marathon? And not in the Special Olympics, but against fully able-bodied athletes? This guy I had to meet.

As I learned, Jim, who was then twenty-eight, had lost his leg six years before while studying acting at Yale, where he had a football scholarship. One day, while riding his Honda motorcycle through a busy intersection, he was hit by a bus that had run a red light. "The bus basically ran over me," Jim told me. "My heart stopped in the ambulance and again in the operating room." Jim described to me how, six days later when he came out of his coma, he looked down and discovered that his left leg was gone. He talked to me, quite intimately, of how he had coped psychologically and physically with his injury.

I looked at him. Jim was tall, six foot five, ruggedly handsome, with blue eyes and jet-black hair. He was making inroads in his acting career and had already landed a part on *Days of Our Lives.* The loss of his leg didn't inhibit him in any way; in fact he rather flaunted it. He never resorted to a cosmetic limb that might mask his handicap; his prosthesis was an uncovered steel rod, and he never hesitated to wear shorts.

He devoted all his spare time to athletic training to prove his handicap would not hold him back. He was now competing in triathlons, sometimes called Ironman contests — running, bicycling and swimming — a grueling sport that is daunting for even the most able-bodied athletes.

Suddenly, the hero of my new novel got a new face — Jim's face.

We became friends, and his friendship and advice became especially welcome when a couple months after our meeting I found myself recovering in the aftermath of the helicopter crash.

We talked a lot. I could confide in him the guilt that I felt about Lee and David. I had lived, but they had died — and at such a young age. Jim was understanding. "We don't control everything," he reminded me. "The Man Upstairs has a lot to do with it."

I was surprised by his clear understanding of life's unfathomable puzzles. I myself wasn't grasping it at all. But he made me realize that there is a spiritual aspect to life that I had been ignoring. And then something totally inexplicable happened to Jim.

I'm getting ahead of myself, but I have to tell you the rest of his story. At the beginning of June 1993, Jim felt he was in his best shape ever, and he invited me to watch him race a triathlon in Mission Viejo, California. I couldn't make it, but suggested that he come up to L.A. afterward and spend a few days with me. Jim agreed.

My hero Jim
MacLaren,
who overcame
all odds.

It was the last day of the race. Jim had just finished a strong two-mile swim. Hunched over the handlebars of his bicycle, he was racing down the streets of a suburban neighborhood, when a police officer, obviously not realizing how fast he was going, waved a van through. There was no way Jim could stop. The van hit his rear wheel. Jim was thrown through the air and struck a lamppost head-first.

When I got the call, I rushed to the hospital. Jim was lying motionless in intensive care, a steel halo screwed into his head. He had broken his spine.

His eyes darted toward me as I came into the room. "Kirk, what are the chances of something like this happening twice in eight years?" His voice had the same resonance, and there was not a hint of self-pity. And then he said, "What am I supposed to learn from this?"

I had to go into the hall to cry.

Before this terrible thing happened to him, Jim had never let his prosthesis stop him. Now he doesn't let his wheelchair stop him. He goes around the country giving motivational speeches. He never makes a morning appointment because he must spend the first half of the day battling his body — waking up nerve endings, gradually coaxing cramped muscles to relax, pushing stiff joints to move again.

I think of Jim a lot when I get up in the morning and my aging body confronts me. Don't tell Jim, but it hasn't stopped me from complaining.

CHAPTER

EIGHT

Six months had passed since the helicopter crash. Had I managed to sublimate the shock of confronting my mortality? Had I buried myself in work and left hanging the hard questions forced on me? Was I complaining too much about my aches and pains, failing to appreciate the very gift of life?

Perhaps all of the above. At any rate, God must have felt a reminder was due.

I was horrified when the doctor looked at my X rays and said, "The atrial wire to your pacemaker is broken."

"Again?" I exclaimed.

Two years before the same wire had been broken and the whole pacemaker had to be replaced; at the time, the blame was put on my pectoral muscles. Apparently pacemakers are generally placed in inactive people whose chests are mounds of immobile fat, or so the doctor said. I am quite active; I exercise regularly, and the movement of the muscles must have severed the wire. The problem was supposedly fixed when the pacemaker was replaced and relocated. So what was it this time?

The doctor speculated that it probably happened in the crash, but he was not sure that it was a good idea to mess with the pacemaker for a third time.

I was depressed. The next day I was to head for Nova Scotia to start filming the TV movie *The Secret*, and the medical examination of my bionic parts was one of the insurance criteria for the movie. What would happen now?

I called Dr. J. Warren Harthorne in Boston, a specialist who had examined me less than a year before. It was reassuring to hear him say, "Kirk, go off and do your movie, you'll be all right with just the ventricle wire." He explained that the atrial wire was a safety and that the ventricle wire was the important one.

I was relieved. But the insurance company was not. They set an outrageous premium, I guess fearing that the lone wire would give out and I'd kick the bucket during the movie.

The producer, Robert Halmi Sr., couldn't afford the premium, but he decided to hire me without insurance. He was very brave. The same thing had happened to Burt Lancaster — as a result of bypass surgery — but the producers of his movie, *Old Gringo*, in which he was to star with Jane Fonda, decided they could do without Burt and the expensive insurance. They hired someone else, Gregory Peck. Halmi could have done the same; he risked a lot with me.

Fortunately, everything went well and I completed the movie without a hitch. (I have done several movies since then with one wire. I feel like a bird flying on one wing.)

I was very grateful to Halmi, an old friend from way back. When I first met him some thirty years ago, he was a photographer assigned to accompany me on my first (and only) wild-game hunt — the most stupid thing I've ever done. But, at the time, I was gung-ho, buying all the proper paraphernalia, checking guns and racing off into the wilds of Kenya.

They nicknamed me Killer Douglas. I was drunk with power as I softly pulled the trigger of my high-powered rifle and watched a leopard, a gazelle, an oryx, a zebra and other defenseless animals fall to the ground. Halmi photographed these "heroic" endeavors, and you can see them if you like in a book called *Great Hunts*. In it you can read about Killer Douglas along with the Shah of Iran, King Paul of Greece, Prince Bernhard of the Netherlands and other swell guys.

The trophies I brought back were proudly mounted on the wall of my projection room. And then one day I realized how obscene it was and got rid of them. Later, I learned that as a Jew I had committed a sin. It is against my religion to hunt and kill wild animals, let alone eat them.

Of course, none of this was Halmi's fault. He was pulling the trigger on a camera, not a gun. But I guess he got sick of it, because he went into making movies instead and became a very successful, award-winning producer.

Back when he was first getting started in the movie business, I lent him a thousand dollars; he paid it back, but in hindsight I should have let him keep it and taken stock in his company instead. It has become a very large company, winner of numerous Emmys, producing some of the very finest movies you see on cable and network television.

The Secret was one of them. It was the story of a man who all his life has managed to cover up the fact that he never learned to read. He never knew the reason — that he had dyslexia. When his young grandson begins having trouble in school, the grandfather must face, and publicly admit, his own problem in order to get the little boy the help he needs.

I was very touched by the story. I had a particular interest in dyslexia because my son Joel suffers from it. I agreed to do it.

The best part of making *The Secret* was working with ten-year-old little Jesse Tendler, who played Danny, my grandson. One day during the filming, it suddenly struck me that Danny was Issur's age. Issur still lived inside of me, and a part of me was still ten years old too. But I was playing the part of a *grandfather*, and in real life I *was* a grandfather.

Maybe because I was playing the part of an old man who is forced to deal with a problem he has had since childhood, I began to wonder if my allegiance to Issur was not a problem too. I sensed that it weakened me. It prevented me from really growing up and being a complete man.

Of course, in the movies I could pretend I was a man. And if you made many movies, like I did, you played the role of a man a good part of the time.

Many stories have been written about my zeal to overcome poverty, make it to college (on a truck-load of fertilizer), work my way through dramatics school and so on. The line from *Champion* was often used to describe me: "From the depths of poverty, he rose to become champion of the world." Like Midge Kelly I was seen as someone who had punched his way to stardom. All my life people have admired my "machismo," my vitality. What energy! What will to succeed!

Not true!

I was no champion. I was acting out the role of someone I wanted to be. Faking it to make it. I saw myself quite differently — as a very passive person, lacking in ambition.

I remember little Issur walking away from Eagle Street, going down to an open field not far from the carpet mills. I see him lying down in the tall grass next to a pond close enough for him to reach over and let his fingers ripple through the water. Little Issur looks up at the blue sky. He is removed from everything. He is nothing and he likes it. He lies there and recites his favorite poem:

> *I wish I were a little rock a-setting on a hill,*
> *Doing nothing all day long but just a-setting*
> *   still.*
> *I wouldn't eat, I wouldn't sleep, I wouldn't*
> *   even wash;*
> *I'd just set still a thousand years and rest*
> *   myself by gosh.*

That poem has stayed with me for about seventy years. Being a rock is such a luxury. It feels good to be nothing, not even to dream. Just to sink into the earth. But becoming a rock is not a luxury that I gave myself often in life. It seems to me that my whole life was devoted to denying myself that indulgence, pushing myself as hard as I could, all the while fantasizing about becoming a nice little old rock.

In a way, the helicopter crash delivered a big dividend — now I could become a rock. My back was aching, my knees were stiff, sometimes it was too painful to move. I had a good excuse to fulfill my long-standing ambition. But now that I could be a rock, it was the last thing I wanted to be. So much for childish fantasies. Remember the old saying: Be careful what you wish for — it might come true.

Is this a problem that all men face? If so, I hope that most men grow up before they are seventy. But then, let me tell you, you never completely grow up. Nor should you. Some of your childlike qualities — curiosity, the yearning for adventure, the hunger to learn and experience new things — help keep you vital and young. The trick is keeping it all in balance. Figuring out how to grow up without growing old. It's a never-ending struggle, a continuous process subject to the laws of mutability — constant change, constant growth. And if you stop growing, you die.

Long before I grew up I became a father. Being a father is a terribly difficult job, especially when you are not completely grown up yourself.

I have four sons from two marriages. My oldest

son is now fifty-two, the youngest thirty-eight. Not children anymore, not for a long time. But in the years that they were small I had to remind myself that I was a father, because often I didn't feel like one. I wanted to be a son and have a father. I felt cheated.

My father had rarely been around. I resented being left at the house with my six sisters and my mother, while my father went off into the world of men. I tried to peek into his world — the saloon . . . the rough voices of men . . . smoke . . . clinking of glasses. I couldn't see much because the windows were painted with some design to obscure the view within. If you were very tall, you could peek over into that womb for grown-up men who had left their families behind. Was it too tough for them to be husbands and fathers? With

My sons, Eric, Michael, Joel and Peter with their father.

71

alcohol and male camaraderie, they reassured one another.

How could I be a father when I had never served out my apprenticeship as a son?

As a result, I often felt inadequate. My role model was not a man who spoke quietly while puffing on his pipe and leaning back in his chair. Pa was a wild man. The strongest man in town.

Precious to me still are those brief memories of when I won his attention. I'll never forget the day Pa bought me an ice-cream cone after he unexpectedly came into a school auditorium, stood in the back and saw me acting out the role of a shoemaker with his elves. I was eight. Another afternoon, when I was ten, he took me into an empty saloon and bought me a glass of loganberry juice. I looked around. So this was where my father spent almost all his evenings. The bar seemed so high. Dust particles danced in the rays of sunlight shooting through the cracks in the window shade. Years later, playing a scene in a saloon for *Gunfight at the O.K. Corral*, I thought about that afternoon.

When I first started writing my autobiography, *The Ragman's Son*, I expected to produce what I thought my fans would be interested in — the story of a "movie star." Instead, I found myself writing about an unhappy child who never got a pat on the back from his father. And I discovered that I had never left my childhood. I still carried it with me, buried deep down. Often, I would ignore it . . . try to run away from it . . . get rid of it . . . kill it. But it was no use — it was always there.

Through Issur, I relived the feeling of being vulnerable and small and surrounded by giants. All grown-ups seemed to be so tall, so big, with loud voices. They could kill you. Sometimes Issur wanted to kill them. The biggest battle that he fought was with Pa.

On one of the rare occasions when my father ate with us, we were all sitting around the table drinking hot tea in a glass, Russian style. Pa held a sugar cube between his teeth and slurped the tea through the sugar. He sat there, big and strong, sullenly ignoring us all. The more I looked at him, the weaker I felt, until I was sure I would die if I didn't do something. Suddenly, I stood up — David facing Goliath. I filled a spoon with hot tea from my glass.

My father, Harry, the toughest guy
in Amsterdam, New York.

My sisters were all looking at me, holding their breath. I took the spoon carefully in my hand, and I flicked it across the table, right into my father's face. He let out a roar like a lion, reached across the table and grabbed me, lifted me up and flung me through a door into the next room. I landed on a bed. I'd like to think that he was aware that the bed was there.

I was triumphant. I had risked death and I had come out alive. I always look back at that as one of the most important moments of my life. I knew that flicking that teaspoon of tea in his face set me apart from my six sisters. For so long I had felt like the odd duck among them. Now I had defined myself as a man. Now my father couldn't ignore me. At that moment, he knew I was alive.

Now the hero of my life would pay attention to me, now he would rescue me from the women, take me with him into the world of men. But he never did.

For so long I saw my father as powerful, frightening, gnashing his teeth or yelling words that came out as a rumble of thunder. It took me forty years to realize that my father — "the strongest man in town" — was really weak, frightened and insecure. He was unable to deal with seven squalling kids, and with a wife who was always calm, quiet and patient, all the things he wasn't, which only made him feel even more inadequate and forced him to escape to the nearest saloon. How pathetic.

I am embarrassed now, rereading *The Ragman's*

Son, how angry I was with him, yet I understand my childish need to express my anger. That anger I was able to express only three times during his lifetime — when I threw the tea in his face, when I refused him a loan, and, most cruelly, when he was dying. He asked me to stay. I said I had to go and see my kids: "You had children and now I have them." I wanted to drive home the point that I was a good father to my kids, unlike him.

But was I a good father? No.

Trying to be a father filled me with tension. It made me uneasy. Once I asked Michael, "Was I a good father?" His answer: "Geez, Dad, you were so tense, so uptight, a wild man."

And yet I longed to be a father who sat back in his chair, puffed on his pipe and spoke softly to his sons. But no writer had scripted that role for me.

When Michael was born in New Brunswick, New Jersey, Diana, my first wife, and I took him home from the hospital. (Oddly enough our home was a real castle; we were staying with Diana's sister Ruth, who had married Seward Johnson of Johnson & Johnson.) We put him in a room next to ours. At night, when he cried, I would rush in frantically, not knowing what to do. But when he was quiet, it was almost worse. I'd keep checking to make sure he wasn't dead.

Diana and I separated when Michael was about five, Joel about three. Toward the end of our marriage I vividly remember Diana and me having a bitter argument in the kitchen. We saw Michael approaching and we stopped. He walked in, sensed the tension and burst out crying. The Issur inside me identified with his pain, yet the adult was at a loss for what to do. There was another time that left a searing picture in my mind. We had already divorced and Michael had come to stay with me. In the evening, when he was supposed to be asleep, I went out. I was walking down the steps to my car and looked up at the window. Michael was peering over the sill and crying. Did he feel abandoned? I felt pangs of guilt, but I drove off.

I had married for the second time — to Anne. We had two sons, Peter and Eric. Now, I was an experienced father. I could play the role. No way. *Aria da capo.* Return to the original theme.

Like my father, I was frightened, so I ran off. But instead of running into the womb of a saloon, I ran off into another world — the imaginary world of movies. I kept myself busy, making one after another. Besides providing a sanctuary, a means of escape from a family where I had no role to play, it was a lucrative way to make a living. It paid the bills and then some. I had to be away a lot, because I was the bread winner. Was that true? Yes and no.

But I am not convinced that it would have made a difference if I had stayed home. I have come to understand that there is a universal principle at work for each of us — whether we grow up in a mill town or in Beverly Hills. Sometime in childhood you are dealt a card, and often the person who deals the card is your parent. The card usually represents a childhood trauma of some sort — your parents are poor, your parents are rich, your parents get divorced, your parents stay together when they should have divorced, your parents neglect you, your parents overpower you with attention, your parents die, you wish your parents died, your parents are perfect, your home life is perfect but then war breaks out in your country, and on and on it goes.

It is guaranteed that something has happened in your childhood that has imprinted you for life, and chances are it is linked to the main fear in your life — fear of abandonment, fear of intimacy, fear of being controlled . . . you fill it in.

The point of all of this is — we are stuck with this card dealt to us in childhood, and everything in life depends on how we play it. The credit or the blame for how the game turns out is all ours.

I should have known that. As an adult, I should not have blamed my father so much. I should have taken more responsibility. I think of my father more now. I am almost the same age as my father was when he died. Suddenly I will catch myself standing in an awkward way, leaning on one hip, and I think, That's how my father used to stand. Did he have a bad back too that I didn't know about?

For the movie *Greedy* I had to wear a mustache and be unshaven most of the time. I would be startled by my face in the mirror. "My God, it's Pa."

If only I could talk to him. It's not that I was wrong about him. He drank away what little money he had, deprived his kids of food and insulted his wife. But now I know why he acted the way he did. I understand the despair that drove him to drink. I understand him, just as I hope my sons will understand me and my weaknesses someday . . . and forgive me.

CHAPTER

NINE

While I yearned for my absent father, I took my mother for granted. Even though we were dirt poor, she had managed by the strength of her spirit to create a warm and secure environment for me.

When I was sick, she made "goggle-muggles" — ah, how I loved those concoctions of raw eggs and butter in hot milk. When I was scared, she told me stories about angels. Years later I put those stories in a children's book called *The Broken Mirror.* The hero of the book, Moishe, was modeled after Issur, of course.

She tried her best to teach me that I was special; that I was a man. I remember one instance in particular. I see her in my mind now, squatting down to pluck a chicken. I squat down next to her and watch. And suddenly she says in Yiddish, "A boy is a boy, but a girl is *dreck*." That startled me, but it didn't make me feel any better.

Oh Ma, Ma. I did not appreciate you. I lumped you with my six sisters and thought of you as part of a gaggle of women who were trying to overwhelm my budding masculine identity. I'm sorry, I'm so sorry.

My mother was a wonderful woman who gave me my best qualities. It just took me a long time to

My mother, Bryna, who taught me
gentleness and compassion.

become conscious of that. But my heart knew it always. It is no accident — I see now — that when I formed my independent production company back in the early 1950s, I named it after my mother, Bryna.

It was the name my father never called her; to him she was always "Hey you," or "the missus." But Bryna was the name I taught her to write. Before that she always signed my report cards from school with an X.

My mother was illiterate — in English. But I remember how on the Sabbath she would make our whirlwind family stand still, and sit on the porch reading her Hebrew prayer book.

After the Bryna Company had become famous producing hits like *Paths of Glory* and *The Vikings*

80

(and later *Spartacus*, *Lonely Are the Brave* and *Seven Days in May*), I took her to Times Square one night in a big limo and pointed out a sign that covered the whole building. "You see, Ma, in lights, BRYNA PRESENTS . . ." My mother shook her head and sighed, "America, such a wonderful land." I agreed with my mother.

It is no coincidence that when I formed the Bryna Company, I also started a charitable foundation. I should have named it after my mother as well, because it was clearly her influence that was playing out in me.

I remember that in our home we had a small tin box — a *pushke* — nailed to the wall. *Pushke* in Yiddish means tin can, but this one was more like a piggy bank. It was where we placed coins to be given to charity. Of course, we had barely enough to eat, so our *pushke* was never bulging. But my mother made sure that something was always in it. The Torah commands us to give to the poor. Charity is called *tzedaka* — justice. And even a beggar must give *tzedaka,* because there is always someone who has less.

We lived near the railroad tracks, and often hobos would come to the door begging for food. My mother always found something to give them.

A lot of people in the neighborhood thought she was a *tzaddikes* — a saint. They would bring her a handkerchief to bless and then place it on the head of some sick person, convinced that her blessing would make the sick well. Maybe it did.

My freshman year in college, I became ill with

81

Drowning among the women of my family,
my sisters and mother.

the flu, and was lying in my dormitory room with a high fever. There was a knock on the door: "Your mother's on the phone." I was startled — we didn't have a telephone at home. She never called. I threw on a robe and walked down the hall.

My mother was calling me from a neighbor's home. "I had a feeling you were sick," she said. After assuring her that I would be fine, I went back to my bed perplexed. How could she have known?

I never gave her credit for so many things she did and was responsible for. Only now I realize the profound influence she had on me.

Most of all, I remember vividly how she died. She had been in the hospital for some time, unable to fight off pneumonia because of her weak heart and complications from her diabetes. My sisters and I stayed at her side as she got weaker and weaker, drifted in and out of consciousness. At dusk one day she roused herself. "What day is it?"

"Friday, Mama."

"Don't forget to light the candles for the Sabbath."

We quickly brought four candles to the room and started to light them. The nurses came in screaming. With the oxygen in the room, we could have blown up the hospital. So we went to my sister Betty's house to do it there. Afterward, I came back alone.

I was overwhelmed by my mother's composure and dignity. My father had died some years before, and the look in his dying eyes was unmistakable — sheer terror.

Watching my mother in that hospital bed, I must have seemed pretty scared myself, because she looked up at me and smiled a clear, serene smile. It was the same kind of smile she used to have every Sabbath when she sat on the porch with her prayer book. "Don't be afraid, Issur. It happens to all of us," she said.

I choked. Holding my own breath, I watched my mother breathe so slowly, in, then out, each breath causing her pain. Until a long, deflating exhale followed by . . . nothing.

That's how the *tzaddikim* die, I have been told. It is called "dying by the kiss of God." The same God who created man by breathing life into him now kisses him and takes that breath away. It is a sign from God that someone is very special. Moses died that way, the Bible says.

I think a lot about how my mother died. I have not been a *tzaddik;* I cannot expect to die in this special way. But I do not want to go terrified into the darkness.

Five years of therapy helped me to become aware of the fact that all my life I have been seeking a replacement for my mother among the women with whom I formed relationships. I have something psychologists call a "mother complex."

I constantly sought from the women around me a mother substitute — I wanted to be taken care of, I wanted to be passive, I wanted them to make the decisions for me. Issur, the little boy with his baggage of needs, somehow prevented me from making my own decisions, caused me to become overdependent on others. He interfered with my life — often in such simple ways.

For years, I never carried a key to my house. Little boys don't carry keys. They knock on the door and someone allows them to come in. A few years ago, I decided to carry a key. People in my household — my wife and my two housekeepers, Concha and Fifi — looked at me with surprise; their eyes widened as I walked through the door. And I had a feeling of doing an amazing thing, carrying the key to the house that I owned.

When I realized the power that comes from growing up, I craved more of it. Finally, it hit me. Issur was the whole problem. There was no longer any doubt in my mind — Issur must go! He allowed people around me to infantilize me. Clinging to Issur made me feel like going back to my mother's kitchen — a warm, secure place that I loved, a place with no responsibilities. But I knew I had to run away from it, just as I had to run away from Amsterdam.

I could see how Issur was holding me back. I didn't want to be a "boy" all my life. I wanted to be a man.

It was Issur's fault. I became more and more angry with him. I began to see him as my foe. He had to be destroyed. I tried to find ways of mustering up the courage to kill him.

Visions of Abraham came into my mind. I could see him up on Mount Moriah with a raised knife,

Peter, Michael, me, Anne and Eric at the
dedication of Harry's Haven.
(© Alan Berliner)

85

ready to sacrifice his little boy, Isaac. I was ready too.

It was a tough decision because I was very fond of Issur — such a helpless kid, so vulnerable, and he never meant me any harm.

Then it came to me that Abraham did not kill Isaac, but that he was *prepared* to kill him, for a higher ideal, God. Maybe the willingness to make such a sacrifice was enough. Maybe I would be destroying a part of me that I loved. A part of me that was precious. A part of me that I could not live without. That's when I made the decision. I will not kill Issur, I will keep him within me, I will protect him, I will take care of him, but I will never again let him dominate me. After all, he is a child. A well-meaning child, but still a child. I am a man. And I must be the parent to the child within me.

At last I grew up. When I became an adult who wasn't dependent on his mother or angry with his father, I found that I looked at my childhood in a totally different way. And finally, after a lifetime — discharging all my hurt and rage, inching my way toward an understanding of him — I was able to forgive my father.

But I wanted Pa to forgive me. I went back to my hometown of Amsterdam and visited my father's grave. He is buried in a peaceful cemetery surrounded by huge elm trees, near the bank of a gurgling brook. I put a small stone on his grave, as is custom, recited the kaddish, the prayer said for the dead, and asked him to forgive me for all my harsh thoughts. I felt that he did.

As a symbol of forgiveness, I dedicated an Alzheimer's unit at the Motion Picture Country Home in his honor. No one in my family had that dreadful disease, although my dear friend, the beautiful Rita Hayworth, died from it at sixty-eight. I took over this project, because Alzheimer's is such a tragedy. I called the place Harry's Haven.

People said, "Don't call it Harry's Haven, it sounds like a saloon."

I laughed. "That's where my father spent most of his time. He would approve."

CHAPTER

TEN

Becoming involved with Harry's Haven felt very good. It made me realize how gratifying giving could be. Of course, I had always given to charity; I had even established a charitable foundation of my own back in the 1950s. But I had always dealt with it from a distance. Checks went out to institutions I knew only by name.

What was it that at this late stage in life made me so acutely aware of the plight of people all around me — made me feel it? I don't know. All I know is that my responses were not calculated, reasoned ones; they were impulsive. Maybe I was trying to repay in some small way for having survived that helicopter crash.

But the progress of my foundation seemed slow, the contributions too small. I wanted to do more, give more.

That's when I hit on the idea of selling off my collection of art. Over the years, the works of Picasso, Braque, Soutine, Vuillard, Dubuffet, Miró and many others have come to adorn my walls. They had been hanging there for too long, I decided. Why not sell them?

The first artwork I ever bought was a lithograph by Toulouse-Lautrec. It was 1948; I paid five hundred dollars and gulped when I did it. That was a lot of money to me back then, but I was in Hollywood starting a movie career, so I took the plunge. I liked that lithograph — it was really a poster — and I still have it, a portrait of Aristide Bruant, a singer/actor who ran a bistro in Montmartre frequented by Lautrec. It is a profile of a haughty man wearing a large black cape and a tilted black sombrero set rakishly on the back of his head; an orange scarf is wrapped loosely around his neck and casually tossed over his shoulder. What insecurities lay beneath that voluminous cape? After all, he was an actor; all actors are insecure and shy, though some hide it better than others.

A friend, an actor named Marc Lawrence, helped me make a frame for the lithograph, and I hung it over the stone fireplace in my house. As I admired it back then — nearly fifty years ago — I never realized that I would eventually own an art collection worth millions of dollars.

When I married Anne, she encouraged me to start buying more seriously. She had a fine eye and knew the marketplace, having once worked in a gallery in Paris. I remember I was in Munich in 1960 making *Town Without Pity* when Anne called from California. "The Thompson collection of Picasso is up for sale. Let's buy one." Of course, she had the "one" all picked out — a seated child with a squashed-in face and two eyes on the same side of her head. It was typical of Picasso's work during the thirties. I thought it was awful.

It was early morning and I was still in bed in my room at the Vier Jahreszeiten Hotel. With not much interest, I leafed through the catalogue of Picasso masterpieces that Richard Feigen, an art dealer from New York, had brought over. Nothing here for me, I thought, and then I saw it — a bull on his knees in a ring of pink sand, the matador above him, sword raised high, ready to give him the coup de grace. I felt for that bull; I identified with him. Why? I don't know.

"How much for the paintings?"

"Which?"

"The one Anne likes . . . and this one." I pointed to my bull.

Feigen's eyes widened. He did some rapid calculations. "Eighty-seven thousand dollars."

I gulped.

"It's a bargain," he added.

I bought them both.

Years later, I got a tax assessment for over a million dollars. We didn't have the money. We should have borrowed it; instead we sold the two Picassos for a million dollars. I didn't mind losing the girl with the crushed face. That was Anne's sorrow. But I sure felt a tug on losing my bull. I thought of him often.

Some time later, in New York, I was wandering around the Museum of Modern Art's exhibition of Picassos. I rounded a corner and ran into my bull. That matador still had not delivered the fatal blow. I asked the curator if it was possible to buy it back, but he said that the new owner, some guy from

Switzerland, definitely wouldn't sell.

"By the way," I asked, "what is the value of that painting?"

"About four million."

I gulped. It seems that I was always gulping when I heard the price of a painting.

"And how much for the girl?"

"The seated child? The one you used to have?"

"Yeah."

"About six million."

Yes, I gulped again. Who the hell decides what a painting is worth?

One day I became angry. A visitor standing in my living room in front of a large Dubuffet said, "That's worth about three million dollars."

I looked at him in disbelief.

"Yes," he said, "art prices are going up."

I thought about it for a long time, and then I made a decision.

"Anne," I said to my wife casually, "let's sell our paintings."

She looked at me, clearly perplexed. "Why?"

"I think it's wrong for us to have that much money hanging on the wall."

"But if we sell them, we'll have to pay large capital-gains taxes."

"We won't pay the taxes."

"What are you talking about?"

"We'll give the money away."

"You are crazy."

"No, we'll put it in a charitable foundation."

And we did — at a terrible price to Anne. She

missed those paintings tremendously, much more than I did.

But it's not easy to sell paintings. Let me tell you about it.

Provenance. That's an important word in the art world. It means the place of origin, the chain of ownership, the validity of the painting. For most of our paintings there was a detailed record, but not for one Vuillard that I liked very much. It was a typical homey scene of a woman sitting in an armchair bathed by the light coming from a lamp on the table. The provenance? It had been owned by a director of an important museum before us, and we had bought it through Richard Feigen. The auction people at Christie's suggested that we send a photo of it to Paris for further authentication. The report came back that it was a fake! My wife and I were astounded. How could that be? We had bought it from an established art dealer who got it from a museum director. Who the hell is this guy in Paris making this judgment from a photo?

I was dumbfounded to learn that the Vuillard expert had once been my assistant in Paris while I was there shooting the movie *Act of Love* back in 1953. I never realized he had anything to do with the world of art. But guess what? His father had been the acknowledged expert on Vuillard until he died. Then my former assistant, as his son, inherited that title. Those French genes must really be something. No matter, a cloud descended over that painting.

Then another painting had a problem. One by

Clave, not a very famous artist. It was a large painting of a misshapen girl, composed from cubes, holding a bird cage. It reminded me of that kooky Picasso painting we sold years ago, except I actually liked this girl with her crazy hat. It too needed further provenance. A color photo was sent to the artist in Paris. He determined that it was his work but someone had distorted the girl's cheek. However, he would make it right. We crated it carefully and shipped it to him. Months later it came back. Apparently he had fixed the cheek, though I never could see the difference. But at least now it has a proper provenance, by the artist himself.

But can you trust the artist himself?

Elmyr de Hory was a famous art forger. His forgeries of many artists even now reside in famous homes and museums. One of his better fakes was a rendering of a portrait in the style of Kees van Dongen. An art dealer took the portrait to van Dongen himself, then in his eighties and living in the south of France, to establish provenance. The artist looked at the forgery with a wistful smile as he recounted how many times he had to interrupt the work on this painting to make love to the model.

Elmyr de Hory was able to paint in the style of many great artists and was a genius in his own right. There have been others like him. Some of their fake paintings have since become recognized for their artistry.

I had two de Hory fakes, one a "van Gogh," one a "Monet." I thought they were very good and wanted to hang them in my office. My wife objected adamantly and put them in the cellar. I rescued them and gave them to my son Peter, who admired them very much. He hung the "Monet" in the living room in his house in Montecito. It is a painting of a beautiful young woman in a white dress sitting under a tree. Guests come in and admire it, surprised to find such a "valuable" painting in his house. Peter does not lie; he says, "Dad gave it to his granddaughter Kelsey."

I am fascinated by fakes. After all, what is real, what is beautiful? The top bidder decides. If a forgery is done so well that it confounds the experts, doesn't it have artistic merit? There was recently a story in all the papers reporting that Rembrandt put his name to paintings that he had not done. *The New York Times* headline read, MUSEUM'S REMBRANDTS MAY NOT BE AUTHENTIC. Rembrandt! After all these years, "experts" have dredged up questions about the authenticity of certain Rembrandt paintings at the National Gallery of Art in Washington. A new mystery — who painted them? The Dutch master? Another artist? A combination?

They decided that two of the paintings are the works of his students (with his signature), while a couple of others were done by him with the aid of his students. On others they are still undecided, as they walk up and down clucking their tongues and peering at the artworks with magnifying glasses. But they cannot lift the cloud that now hangs over the Dutch master. So please be careful if you are planning to buy a Rembrandt.

The biggest spur to my interest in art came when I played van Gogh in the biographical film *Lust for Life*. The role affected me deeply. I was haunted by this talented genius who took his own life, thinking he was a failure. How terrible to paint pictures and feel that no one wants them. How awful it would be to write music that no one wants to hear. Books that no one wants to read. And how would you like to be an actor with no part to play, and no audience to watch you. Poor Vincent — he wrestled with his soul in the wheat field of Auvers-sur-Oise, stacks of his unsold paintings collecting dust in his brother's house. It was all too much for him, and he pulled the trigger and ended it all. My heart ached for van Gogh the afternoon that I played that scene.

As I write this, I look up at a poster of his "Irises" — a poster from the Getty Museum. It's a beautiful piece of art with one white iris sticking up among a field of blue ones. They paid a fortune for it, reportedly $53 million. And poor Vincent, in his lifetime, sold only one painting for 400 francs or $80 today. This is what stimulated my interest in buying works of art from living artists.

I want them to know while they are alive that I enjoy their paintings hanging on my walls, or their sculptures decorating my garden: James Rosenquist, Robert Graham, Richard DiRosa, Billy Al Bengston, Chuck Arnoldi, Jim Dine, Joel Shapiro, Sam Francis, Yoram Raanan, Robert Rauschenberg.

My wife met a painter in Paris whom she

admired named Robert Combas. His unusual painting hangs in our entranceway. It is called *Carpe Diem* — "Seize the Day."

That's my motto now. I have been spared, and I don't want to waste any part of the preciousness of life that has been given to me. I want to get out of life all that I can. And I want to help the future van Goghs, whose works adorn my home, do the same — now.

CHAPTER

ELEVEN

Selling artwork, devoting time to charitable causes, writing novels, are all worthwhile means of occupying your time when good scripts aren't coming your way. But then, in the spring of 1993, one did.

It was called *Wrestling Ernest Hemingway*, a story of a growing friendship between two old men dealing with the twilight of their lives. The script spoke directly to me — here were some of the things that I was trying to cope with in my life. I loved it. It was written by Steve Conrad, a young man — only twenty-one years old! — and yet he had an amazing understanding of old people. It was brilliant, and the part of Frank, the vulnerable drifter who pretended to be macho, was perfect for me.

Robert Duvall had been cast in the other part, Walter, the shy Cuban barber, and that made me happy. He's such a fine actor. The director was Randa Haines, best known for *Children of a Lesser God*. I had never worked with a woman director and looked forward to that new experience.

I was happy. I had read so many bad scripts lately and then, just as I was prepared for yet another disappointment, this came along. I couldn't wait to get started.

What excitement an actor feels when he is given

a part that he is dying to play! It never changes, no matter how long you've been a star; it's just the same as when you were starting out and ready to pounce on that choice role guaranteed to get you noticed.

I still remember all the parts I yearned to play that I didn't get. All the times I went to auditions and heard them say, "Too short," or "Too tall," or "Not right."

Somehow your memory of rejection is always the sharpest. I wince thinking about those times. A kid out of dramatic school, I went to see an agent who I hoped would represent me. His office was a dilapidated hole-in-the-wall, but I was sure he had the ticket to my future. After I gave him my pitch, I was thrilled to hear the magic words, "Okay, okay . . . come back Tuesday and read a scene." I went home and worked on my lines. And then I came back for my big break. Standing before his desk, I started my scene with full emotion as he leaned back in his chair. The phone rang. He picked it up. I stopped. "No, no, go ahead," he said. He had me continuing the scene while he talked on the phone. When he hung up, he dismissed me with, "Yeah, well, I'll let you know." And, of course, I never heard from him again.

None of us likes being rejected. Rejection says: "I don't want you. I don't like you." We've all applied for jobs we didn't get. But I think rejection is much more intense for an actor because it is *you* who are being rejected. It is such a personal thing. They don't want *you*. It's like asking a girl you have a crush on for a date and being told, in one way or another, "Buzz off."

When you are first starting out, you try to become immune to it, but you never can quite succeed — you get hurt each time. Finally, if you're lucky, you become a star. Now you don't have to audition. You are accepted. You are offered the part, and that's that. You are the one who says yes or no. And you say no a lot, because you are offered many bad parts. But once in a while something truly special comes along — something like *Wrestling Ernest Hemingway.*

I called my agent, Fred Specktor at CAA, trying to restrain my excitement. "That's the part for me."

"Yes, you'd be terrific, but . . ." He began to hem and haw. "Warners wants you — Semel and Daly both think you'd be terrific."

"So make the deal."

A long pause. "But the director wants to meet you."

"No problem. I'd like to meet her."

They brought Miss Haines to my home. Our talk went quite well. I told her a little bit about my life, how I identified with the character of Frank in *Wrestling Ernest Hemingway.* She sat there, listening attentively, peering at me over her glasses.

I wanted to impress her even more. I stood up and told her about my father. "He was a Russian peasant, you know — never went to school. He wanted to quit smoking. So how did he do it? He kept a cigarette in his breast pocket. When he felt like smoking, he'd pull out the cigarette and glare at it. 'Who stronger? You? Me? I stronger.' " (All this of course with my father's accent.) "And then he'd put the cigarette back in his pocket."

A brilliant little vignette. She smiled.

My agent called the next day. "She really likes you, Kirk . . . but . . . ah," he started to stutter.

"What?"

"She wants Richard Harris."

I swallowed. Of course, I knew Richard well. I'd worked with him. Damn good actor! We did *The Heroes of Telemark* together. "He's very good, but I don't think he is quite right for this part. I think I'm *perfect*."

"Kirk, you know the studio wants you, but she feels that Richard Harris is a better fit."

"So, where are we?"

"Well —" he started to stutter again, but it came out. "You have to test."

"Test?"

"If you want the part you have to test for it."

I couldn't believe it. I hadn't tested for a part since I first came out to Hollywood in 1946 for *The Strange Love of Martha Ivers* with Barbara Stanwyck and Van Heflin.

I had been a stage actor, never in front of a camera before. The director, Lewis Milestone, rehearsed me a couple of times, and then said, "Well, how do you feel?"

I said, "Let's rehearse it one more time."

"Well, okay."

After that rehearsal, he said, "Are you ready now?"

I didn't know how to answer I was so nervous

and scared, but I said, "Yeah."

He said, "Go home. I already shot it."

I was stunned and relieved. He had shot it while I was rehearsing and was a lot less nervous. Of course I didn't know the cameras were rolling. I got the part, and after that I never thought about testing.

But now, almost fifty years later, I had gone full circle.

"But Fred," I said, "there are so many movies that I have done that Miss Haines can look at. Eighty movies!"

"She doesn't care," he said.

I wasn't getting it. "What are you saying?"

"Well, Kirk, what I am saying" — he didn't stutter this time — "is that there is no way you can get the part if you don't test for it."

Yeah, this was insulting — damn insulting. But the more I thought about how much I wanted this part, the less angry I became. What the hell, I said to myself. If you think you're so perfect for the part, Kirk, test for it. Why not?

Randa Haines gave me about ten pages of script — four different scenes, a lot of lines. I put aside the novel I was writing, and I learned my lines. On the appointed day, I went down to the studio early in the morning. I tried to look at it as an interesting experience. I met many of the crew, people that I had worked with on different pictures; they seemed surprised to find me testing for a part. The younger actors who would be playing opposite me (reading the parts that Robert Duvall and Shirley MacLaine were to play) were very deferential. I was embarrassed. I tried to cover it up by joking with them, but I was relieved when Randa Haines showed up and we started.

We worked all day. One scene was especially tough because I had to run backward around the room, and my poor back and knees were killing me. But Randa Haines directed me in a most helpful way. We got along well. When it was over, I was exhausted but happy. That night I prayed that I would get the part.

I waited a few days and heard nothing. Finally, my agent called.

"Well?"

"The studio wants you. They like you. But . . ."

When that "but" comes in, boy, that little word, "but" — what significance it has.

"She still wants Richard Harris for the part."

I tried to stifle the feelings roiling inside of me. I was sorely disappointed. Disappointed? Crushed. I wanted to cry.

But instead I said very calmly, "Look, Fred, I've talked with her, I've tested for her. She doesn't want me."

So Richard got the part. I liked Richard. I sat down and I wrote him this note:

Dear Richard:

It's a great role. I would love to have played it. But you will be magnificent. All my best wishes . . .

Then I thought, Don't be a sore loser, Kirk, and I wrote the director a note too:

Dear Randa:
   I want you to know that I thoroughly enjoyed the short time we worked together. You are certainly a talented lady. You have a great script; a wonderful cast. I know you will put the elements together into a great movie. All my best . . .

Very quickly an answer came back from Richard.

Dear Kirk:
   What a very, very thoughtful note! There is no doubt that we can all learn great lessons from you, not only as an actor, and your remarkable achievements, but also as a human being, for your graciousness and generosity . . . Yes, it is a great role, and I am quite certain that there will be many occasions in the long shooting weeks that I will say to myself, What would Kirk have done with this scene? As always, my very best . . .

I never heard from Miss Haines.
I felt at the bottom of the rejection pit. Having already been humiliated, I now was dismissed, ignored.
I was sure that *Wrestling Ernest Hemingway* was going to be a big hit. And I was jealous that I was not a part of it. Jealousy is one of the mean traits

that we develop in our insecure profession. We don't *kvell* over the success of others. Just the opposite — the success of others often brings only envy that it didn't happen to us.

There is a Jewish joke that goes: If you had a good day, you tell your neighbor that you had a bad day. That way, you can be happy and he can be happy. But if you had a bad day, then you tell your neighbor that you had a good day. That way you are miserable and he can share in your misery.

After a while, I put my hurt feelings aside. What the hell, I thought, I might still find the movie that my son Michael and I want to do together. He was looking and I was looking, but it was difficult to find the right script.

Besides, I consoled myself, this was not the worst disappointment I ever had in life. The worst one I remembered all too well. The worst one was when I was cheated out of my pony.

I was nine years old. And I had solved the puzzle. In the newspaper there had been a drawing of a country scene with five hidden faces. The prize for finding them was a pony. I found the faces very quickly, and I circled them and sent them back.

I was so happy, I fixed up the shed near Pa's barn for the pony; I made it all clean, and I built a place to put the hay and found a pail for the oats. And I waited for my pony.

Instead I got a letter saying I won, but first I had to sell ten subscriptions to a magazine.

It was hard, but I did it.

But then I got another letter, saying that I *almost*

won but somebody far away in California got the pony.

Poor Issur. Now *that* was a disappointment!

As I was licking my wounds, my agent called. They had a movie for me to do with Michael. I was excited. But it turned out they meant Michael J. Fox.

It was *Greedy*, a hilarious script written by Lowell Ganz and Babaloo Mandel, the writers of *City Slickers*, *Parenthood*, *A League of Their Own*, and others. It was the story of a wealthy curmudgeon who tests his greedy family to see if anyone of them is worthy to inherit his fortune, if anyone loves him. I was eager to do it.

"They want to meet with you at the producer's office," Fred told me.

Here we go again, I thought. "Maybe they want me to test for the part?" I asked sarcastically.

"No, no," Fred said. "It's just a formality."

I was suspicious. But I went to the office of Imagine, a very successful independent company headed by Ron Howard (once better known as Opie on *The Andy Griffith Show*, now a famous director) and Brian Grazer, his partner. I sat in a chair and tried to be unaware of a dozen pairs of eyes looking at me. They were all so young. They could have been my sons.

It was a pleasant meeting. But at one point as I was talking I saw that I had lost the interest of the producer, Brian Grazer. I stopped, turned to him slowly and said in a deadly voice — "You're not listening."

He almost fell off his chair.

Fred thought the meeting went very well. But the next day he phoned to say that the director wanted to see me privately at my house.

I took a deep breath. "Have they offered me the part?"

"Not yet."

"Then why does he want to meet with me?"

"Kirk, it's just —"

"Yeah, yeah, I know, it's just a formality."

Jonathan Lynn is a very talented director from London. He is also a writer and a very good actor. He told me that he wanted to be sure that he could work with a "legend." He decided he could. It was a short meeting.

Greedy started shooting in a big house, an old

Why is Michael J. Fox wearing a hard hat? The hazards of working with me are many. (*Peter Iovino Photo © Universal Studios, Inc.*)

mansion in Northridge, a part of L.A. County that a few months later became famous as the epicenter of the earthquake.

For so many years in the past, I was the youngest member of the cast. After that, I was at least the contemporary of everyone else. But here I was an old man, playing an old man. Everyone in cast and crew were much younger. I knew I was really old, because they all called me "Mr. Douglas."

"Please call me Kirk," I implored, but it wasn't easy for them.

Making *Greedy* was a delightful experience. It wiped away the hurt of *Wrestling Ernest Hemingway*. I played my role in an electric wheelchair. It was fun zipping around and making sudden turns, and it was a great help to my sore back and knees.

By the time that *Greedy* was finished, *Wrestling Ernest Hemingway* came out. I was anxious to see it.

The movie was being released in a limited engagement in December in order to qualify for Oscar considerations. I got an Academy preview cassette, locked the door to my room, turned off the phone and glued my eyes to the screen in great anticipation.

But as I watched, I was more and more puzzled. The movie started off lugubriously. What I imagined would be a light, bouncy scene between Harris and MacLaine — two top actors — was slow and dull.

Duvall, an extraordinary performer, played his role brilliantly, but low-key. Harris surprised me by seeming overly dramatic. One actor was in the cellar, the other in the attic. The story of the growing love between the two men never really jelled.

When the movie was over, I was perplexed. How could this have happened? I must be wrong, I told myself. I must be judging it by how I wanted to do the part. But the reviews came in — all devastating. The movie played in a few theaters and disappeared. How sad!

So much work goes into the making of a film. A young writer poured out his heart and wrote a great script. A lot of money had been spent. Top actors were hired. So who was to blame? It was "A Randa Haines Film." The concept, says the auteur theory, belongs to the director. So Randa Haines screwed it up.

This director interviewed me, made me test, rejected me, but then — the end of the story should be — came up with an Oscar-winning picture. Instead, disaster.

Of course, nobody sets out to make a bad movie, although sometimes I wonder. But Randa Haines has talent. Who knows — she might come up with another great script and ask me to test.

So what's the moral of the story? Be grateful for unanswered prayers. God has a sense of humor. Sometimes He looks down as we pray, and He laughs: "How can I tell this guy that *Wrestling Ernest Hemingway* is gonna be a flop? How can I tell this guy that the nicest thing I am doing for him is not to answer his prayers?"

One thing I have learned — God always answers our prayers, but sometimes the answer is no.

CHAPTER

TWELVE

When I think back over the eighty-some movies I've made, I have to admit that I would make a poor insurance risk — I died in over twenty of them. In *Champion* I was beaten to death in the boxing ring; in *Spartacus*, I was crucified; in *Lonely Are the Brave*, I was hit by a truck hauling toilets; in *Amos*, cancer got me; in *Queenie*, I passed out — or shall I say, passed away — on a park bench along the Thames River. In *Detective Story*, *The Brotherhood* and *The Last Sunset* (to name just three) I was shot, and in *Lust for Life* I shot myself. So, perhaps director John Landis chose me to play Sylvester Stallone's dying father in *Oscar* because I had so much experience.

At first I wasn't interested because the role was a cameo, but John was persistent. "Just read the first five pages of the script," he said.

I could do that much. I read the first five pages and called my agent. "I'll do it."

I couldn't resist. My one and only scene, the opening of the movie before the titles, was a gem. Picture this: My character, an old Italian papa, is on his deathbed. Enter his son Angelo (Stallone), a mob boss, with his henchmen, and he kneels at Papa's bedside.

"My son . . . come closer," I say in a weak voice.

Stallone leans over me.

"Closer."

Stallone is inches from my face.

Crack. I give him a solid smack on the side of his head.

"Papa, what have I done?"

"You gangster! You lie . . . you steal . . . you shoot people!"

"I don't shoot people." Angelo points to his henchmen. "They shoot people."

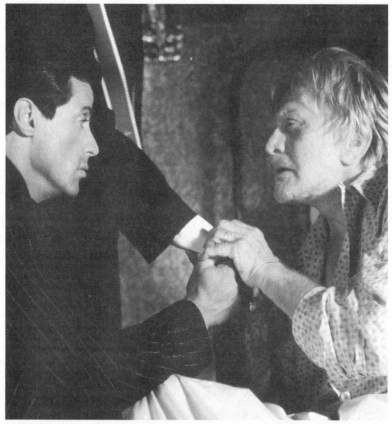

I am exhausted from slapping Sylvester Stallone in *Oscar.* (© *Touchstone Pictures*)

"Shadappa your mouth . . . You bringa shame to da family."

As the scene continues, I extract a promise from him to go straight. Finally, I close my eyes. Stallone, teary-eyed, leans over again to kiss his dying father, when suddenly I come to life.

Crack right across the face.

Angelo is shocked.

"Atsa so you don't forget."

I die.

As we were rehearsing the scene, Stallone was wonderful. He said, "Don't hold back. I can take it."

So I followed instructions. I spent the morning slapping Stallone's face, having a good time.

Later, at a dinner in my honor, Stallone joked that when the director wanted to do another take, he refused. "I'm getting brain damage," he had complained.

Soon after *Oscar* I got another offer to do a death scene, although this one the writer managed to stretch into a full-length motion picture. It was called *Take Me Home Again.*

Reading the script, I realized that it was something I had read before. Some years back, my son Michael had brought me this story of a reunion between a dying father and his wayward son as a possible project for the two of us. At that time, I thought it was too downbeat, but since then it had been rewritten and much improved with a lot of humor and wit added.

I called Michael to say that we should take

another look, but at that time he was tied up making *Disclosure* with Demi Moore. The producers of *Take Me Home Again* wouldn't wait — the project had funding and the green light of NBC — so I agreed to go ahead with Craig T. Nelson (of *Coach* fame) playing the part of the son who "kidnaps" his dying father from a suffocating family and takes him on a wild cross-country trek to find the bed in which the old man was born and in which he wants to die. The "happy" ending to the story is that they succeed in their mission — they find the bed, and the old man gets his wish.

After the movie came out, I was interviewed by a newspaper reporter about it. "Did you find it difficult to play the death scene?" he asked me.

"Do you mean — at my age?" I shot back, leaving him stuttering.

But it was a good question. Since the helicopter crash, I thought often of dying. But for me, it still felt far from reality; death remained in the world of make-believe. Occasionally when a younger person would give me a hand to help me up or down steps, I'd resent it. In filming *Take Me Home Again*, there were some action scenes, like climbing down from a second story using a rope ladder. I insisted on doing these scenes myself.

There was also a scene of me wrestling with Craig, who is about six foot five. I told the director I could do it. But after shooting the scene, my back hurt like hell and I complained.

The director said, "Well, Kirk, you said you could do it."

Take Me Home Again was one long death scene. Craig T. Nelson made it fun. *(Gary Null © 1994 National Broadcasting Company, Inc.)*

"Yeah, I said I could do it once. I didn't know how many takes you had in mind!"

Of course, I was disappointed not to be doing this movie with Michael. But the disappointment was lessened by the pleasure of working with Craig. He is a brilliant actor and a lot of fun to work with.

When we played the final scene — me dying in that bed — I was surprised to see how emotionally affected the cast and crew were. Some were crying. Not because of my superb acting, but because it conjured up images of someone close to them who had died.

I was seventy-seven years old when I played that death scene. Was it a rehearsal for reality? It suddenly struck me that I had just been cast in a whole string of movies playing old, dying men — and I wasn't using much makeup! How the hell did I get from there to here?

"Golden lads and girls all must, / As chimney-sweep-ers, come to dust." I remember reading those pretty lines of Shakespeare when I was young. What a touching sentiment, I thought; how poignant to think of young laughing boys and girls growing old. But that happens to other people, not me.

Vivid in my mind is the memory of a boyhood friend pointing out to me a fifty-year-old man. My jaw dropped — I looked at him in wonder — fifty! A half a century! Now my son Michael — a sexy heartthrob — is fifty-two.

At what time in life are you "getting older"?

I remember I was about forty-five and in peak condition, Michael was sixteen, and we were sitting around the pool of my old house on Canon Drive. I was feeling chipper. The movie I was doing at the time, *Spartacus*, was going very well. "Hey, Mike, how about a race."

"Sure, Dad. Across the pool and back?"

"Okay."

And on the count of three we started. I was swimming as fast as I could. But I couldn't lose my son. He was right up there with me. Coming back, he touched the side of the pool just before I did. But I said, "I won."

Michael was furious. "No, you didn't, Dad. I won."

"It was close, Mike. But I won," I lied.

"Okay," he said. "Let's race again." And he poised himself, ready to take off.

I was still huffing and puffing. "I think you won," I admitted.

Ah, to be forty-five again — or even sixty-five — or seventy-five!

The other day I ran into an actor whom I had worked with some years ago. I was shocked. He had gray hair, lines in his face, wore thick glasses, was hunched over. "My God," I said to my wife, "how old John looks." Then the thought hit me: Does John go home and say the same thing to his wife about me?

I'm shocked when I see a current photo of myself. Is that *me?* What did you expect to see, Kirk — Champion? Spartacus? Doc Holliday walking alongside Burt Lancaster?

But I don't feel old. I feel like the best of life is still ahead of me.

In the Torah, all the patriarchs lived to ripe old ages — most of them died somewhere in their hundreds. Abraham became circumcised at ninety-nine, and after that he sired Isaac. Moses climbed Mount Sinai when he was eighty. I could do that too.

One day, while I was ruminating like this, my son Peter came into the room.

"Peter, do you think I'm old?"

"Hey, Dad. You work out every day, and you look a lot younger than people half your age."

A bit of a hyperbole, but I accepted it.

"But Dad . . . your clothes . . ."

"Huh? Your mother picks out my clothes."

"They look like they came out of a geriatric thrift store."

"How can you say that? Your mother was voted

the best-dressed woman three years in a row."

"Yeah, nineteen fifty-four, nineteen fifty-five and nineteen fifty-six."

"She has impeccable taste."

"But Dad, she wasn't voted the best-dressed man."

He had a point.

Michael had been giving me similar advice. He especially criticized the form-fitting sports shirts I was fond of. "They look like something Jack LaLanne might wear." Jack LaLanne was considerably older than I.

The hip way to dress these days, according to the fashion education I received from Peter, was to wear "deconstructive" clothes. "Deconstructive," I have come to learn, really means "sloppy."

At first I objected. I told him that I wouldn't wear what my grandson Cameron — age seventeen — deems fashionable. I hope by the time this book comes out, Cameron's style — wearing baggy pants with the crotch hanging down between the knees and the belt across the rear end — has gone out of fashion.

But finally, I was convinced that I had to update my wardrobe. And, at the urging of my wife, who actually agreed with him, I submitted to going shopping with Peter. We went to The Gap and I tried on a pair of pants he picked out. "They are much too baggy," I told him, but he insisted. "No, no, Dad, they are just the style."

Well, all right, I am going along with this.

I'm standing there with these pants that are so

big and loose it looks like I just had an accident and am carrying a load in the seat of my pants. And he brings out a jacket to match, with shoulders slumping down to my elbows. I grin and bear it. Then come the shoes. I can't believe it. Big and heavy, like boots. When I was a kid, farmers used to wear shoes like this, with big rubber soles, just perfect for trekking through slop.

"Peter, are you kidding?"

"No, Dad, this is what's in."

The only positive thing I can see about those shoes is that those thick rubber soles make me an inch taller.

"You look perfect," he is saying.

I look at myself in the mirror. Disaster.

But Peter is keeping up the refrain. "That's it. That is the 'in' look. Now you got it."

I didn't say a word to my kid. When I got home, I called the tailor. I had him take in the seat of those pants; I had him cut them down so the ankles wouldn't bag so much. I couldn't do much to alter the shoes.

I've resolved to try to be "with it," but I hope that God rewards me for trying and makes this style go away next year.

I had just appeased my son Peter when another member of my family piped up with a complaint.

It was my wife. "Kirk, you don't hear too well," she said.

I said, "What?"

She said it more strongly. "You don't hear too

well. Do you realize how often I have to repeat myself?"

"It's difficult to hear at a party," I said, "with all that background noise, everybody talking."

But I thought about it and I went down to the House Institute, a big organization that's always hitting me up for money to help poor people hear better (though I never did see a homeless person on the street with a hearing aid).

The doctor took me into a soundproof room, put a pair of earphones on me and asked me to raise my hand when I heard a noise.

For a long time, I heard nothing; then it started to creep in ever so sneakily. *Beep.*

The second I heard anything my hand shot up.

After the exercise was over, and the doctor finished his copious notes, he gave me a report: "Mr. Douglas, you have trouble hearing these sounds." And he started spitting at me: "Sh, ch, ng, kuh, huh, lum, wuh . . ."

It's true — I never heard those words; I don't remember reading them either.

The doctor then took out two hearing aids, loudly proclaiming how tiny they were. They didn't look tiny to me — they looked like two jumbo-size pink olives. He assured me that once placed in my ear, they would be imperceptible to the human eye.

A lie. I've seen pink olives just like that in the ears of President Reagan and Jimmy Stewart.

By the way, at a dinner party Jimmy Stewart or President Reagan is usually seated next to my wife. I think they request it — she's had a lot of practice talking to people who can't hear well.

Jimmy might be saying, "Ronnie, have you been playing much golf lately?"

"What's that? What's that?" asks the president.

Anne, sitting between them, explains. "Have you been playing much golf lately?"

"Every Saturday morning, Jimmy."

Jimmy looks blank.

Anne helps out again. "The president says that he plays every Saturday."

And so it goes. Anne doesn't eat much.

Of what help are those pink olives in their ears? Maybe their tiny batteries are dead. As I learned, inside each pink-olive hearing aid is a tiny battery that can be turned off and on by a tiny key. There is also a teeny-weeny knob that regulates volume.

This was all very difficult for me because I do not have teeny-weeny fingers.

The doctor suggested that I practice wearing them, and with a hearing aid firmly installed in each ear, I left his office. In spite of his assurances, I felt like I had two pink grapefruits protruding from my ears. But I wore them for the ride home.

During the drive, I felt that the volume was either too low or too high, so I kept shifting my hands off the steering wheel to adjust the tiny knobs.

Once at home, I read the manual over very carefully. I learned how to change the tiny batteries with tiny tweezers. That night I went out to a party wearing only one of them. I decided to work up to two gradually. Surreptitiously, I tried to adjust the

Dear Kirk — As always a great pleasure to see you — Warmest Regard
Nancy & Ron

President Ronald Reagan without his
"pink olives."
(*Official White House Photo*)

volume while pretending to be scratching my head.

Well, I had to give it to the doctor. I could now hear sh, ch, ng, kuh, huh, lum and wuh . . . I also heard buzz, fuzz, brrr, grrrr, tizz, wizz and every other background noise imaginable. Sometimes when people greeted me with an embrace, the pressure against my cheek caused the thing to whine in my ear. I found that I was so busy adjusting the hearing aid in order to hear the sound that I lost track of the meaning.

When there was no noise in the room and only one person was talking, I got good results. Like in a movie theater. But I couldn't spend my life in a movie theater.

I went back to the institute for a readjustment.

It didn't help. And that was just the excuse I needed.

So two teeny-weeny hearing aids enclosing teeny-weeny (now probably dead) batteries are sitting collecting dust in my dresser drawer.

Are you chuckling about now?

I hope so. It would be a grim book if, in my attempt to tell you about my confrontation with mortality — and its many repercussions, and (dare I say it?) benefits — I did not inject some humor.

Getting old is not funny, but it's bearable if you can laugh at yourself as you slowly stumble toward your own funeral.

Are we properly serious once again? Okay, so let's move on.

CHAPTER

THIRTEEN

We are all just microscopic specks in a universe without end. We are hurrying and scurrying with our schemes and self-interest. We forget that there is a force that controls our world. Maybe hurricanes, tornadoes, floods and earthquakes are God's ways of reminding us that even though He has given us freedom of choice, there is so much beyond our control. Or maybe they are God's ways of showing that He is displeased with the choices that these little specks are making.

Or maybe it works differently altogether. Maybe our moral choices vibrate out into the physical world and have terrible consequences. Is that idea so crazy? What about the new scientific theories of order and chaos, which tell us that a seagull flapping its wings can start a typhoon? If that is true, then is it not possible that a parent whipping his child might do the same?

We understand none of it. But we do know — because we see it all the time — that no matter how well we lay our plans, something beyond our control can scrap them just like that.

"The best laid schemes o' mice and men / Gang aft agley." Robert Burns was so right!

A young man kisses his fiancée, a stewardess on

TWA flight 800 taking off from Kennedy Airport to Paris. They plan to be married when she returns. Forty-five minutes later she is dead in the Atlantic Ocean along with 229 other people, a victim of an as yet unexplained explosion that ripped the plane apart in seconds.

On January 16, 1994, a little speck called Kirk Douglas was all excited about the imminent publication of his third novel, *Last Tango in Brooklyn*.

I was up in Fillmore getting everything ready for the publicity tour, which would start in New York. In the evening, I took a walk in the citrus groves, stole a few oranges and then, with thoughts for a new book mulling around in my head, I went to sleep. About four-thirty in the morning, the earthquake struck.

God wasn't fooling around. I clung to the mattress as the whole house shook in anger. Everything was pitch black.

Helplessly, I was tossed from side to side. I heard things crashing around me. Finally, after what felt like a half-hour, the quake subsided and I took a deep breath.

"Are you all right?" I yelled out.

Ushi's voice came from her bedroom on the other side of the house: "I'm all right. Stay in bed, the aftershock is coming."

She was right. Within a few minutes, the tremors started again. It was as if God had grabbed the world by the scruff of the neck and had given it a good shake. What message was He delivering?

Maybe this chaos created by the earthquake is

God's way of shaking his finger at the chaos in our world today. Maybe if we can remove the chaos from our lives, nature will be more peaceful too. But if we don't do anything to stop the chaos of Zaire, Bosnia, Somalia, the Middle East, is God going to command nature to match the chaos that we create?

When the aftershock passed, I felt safe enough to sit up in bed and turn on a lamp — nothing.

In the dark, I made myself breathe deeply and try to think clearly. Anne was in Palm Springs, not far away. Where were my sons? Peter and his wife Lisa then lived in Hollywood Hills with my beautiful granddaughter Kelsey. Michael and Eric were in New York. And Joel was in Europe. I groped for the phone and dialed Anne — nothing. I dialed Peter — nothing. Of course, the phones weren't working.

For a long time I lay there in the dark. Finally, when the first light of dawn peeped into the window, I got up and saw that the house was fine, no damage, the crashing noise was just books falling from shelves. I went into the kitchen to make myself some coffee and found Ushi already there muttering that the electric stove wasn't working. The furnace wasn't working either, so we made a fire in the wood stove and cooked breakfast on top of it.

Intermittently I kept trying the phone. With all electricity out and no battery-powered radio, we knew nothing of the damage to the world outside.

I tried the phone again and heard my wife pick it up on the first ring. "Oh, my God," she said. "How are you?" Quickly, we reassured each other. Anne had already been in touch with the kids and knew everyone was okay. But she was worried about me because the epicenter was near Fillmore, and, according to the news, the earthquake had been very severe — 6.6 on the Richter scale.

This is how I learned that part of Route 5 — my usual way home — had come tumbling down. On the other side, Route 23 was closed by a rock slide. And Route 126 was also impassable. I was trapped. But Ushi's little farm was not a bad place to be trapped. The warm morning sun was casting a beautiful glow over the tops of citrus trees. The rooster was crowing; the dogs were begging for treats. The horses were whinnying for their hay.

We took care of them all and then drove into the little town to see what was happening. Ushi's house sits at the foot of the mountains, and perhaps its rock foundation made for firmer ground, or perhaps it was just fate. The town itself — in the sandy valley — was in shambles. One three-story brick building looked as if a giant paw had smashed through its side and clawed off half of it. Down the block, house after house looked as if a scythe had chopped off all the chimneys. Some of the older homes had completely collapsed.

Neighbors were collecting around charcoal grills sharing food — a giant cookout celebrating that the damage wasn't worse. It was amazing to me how a disaster brings out the best in people. A wave of optimism washed over the shock and dismay. They accepted what had happened. No one had lost a life. No one was angry with God.

One enterprising luncheonette owner had set up business in the parking lot of her tiny restaurant. On a charcoal grill pots of coffee were perking, and trays of doughnuts and coffee cakes were laid out on picnic tables. "No charge," said the proprietor as she went about filling Styrofoam cups. I looked around at the mixture of people gathered there — the elderly in their pajamas and bathrobes stood next to Mexican workers — a diverse group brought closer by the catastrophe. There was a camaraderie, a feeling of goodwill. How strange, I thought, that an earthquake should bring people together. Disaster is a great leveler. The earthquake no doubt converted a few atheists too.

Each intermittent aftershock during the day was a reminder of the force of nature. I witnessed one spectacular aftershock that split off the side of a mountain and sent it tumbling down into the valley below, dust rising to the sky like billowing smoke. But, I thought, God is kind. Mankind always bests nature in the contest of destruction. There is enough nuclear power in the world to destroy this planet many times over. Overkill is a fascinating word — how many times can you kill something already dead? We have developed the techniques to annihilate a civilization, but how do you deal with one fanatic? How much more terrifying than the forces of nature is the power of one man carrying a plastic key to paradise who is willing to blow himself up and a bus or a plane full of people along with him?

I had a hectic time, with the phone circuits overloaded, reaching my kids and some close friends. We all just wanted to reassure each other. And then a strange thought entered my mind. How had my friend Burt Lancaster fared during the earthquake? Did he understand what was happening? Burt had had a stroke three years before, which left him completely paralyzed. His movements were so limited, he spent his days in bed or in a wheelchair. He couldn't speak, and no one was sure just how much he understood. Did the earthquake terrify him, or was he perhaps not even aware it happened?

I had not seen Burt since his stroke. His wife, Suzie, didn't want me to visit him. She was afraid that it might upset him to see me. She did not want this once strong physical specimen, now weak and helpless, to see the friend he had often balanced on his shoulders in a song-and-dance routine. Secretly, I thought it would upset *me* to see my friend in such a vegetative state, so I did not quarrel with her wishes.

Every week I would get reports on Burt from Eric Monte, the golf pro, or from Joanna, Burt's daughter. And the report was always the same — no change. Burt couldn't communicate at all; Eric wasn't even sure that he could recognize people.

One day Suzie called to ask me to accept an award for Burt from the Screen Actors Guild. I was glad to do it — Burt played an important role in the union; he always fought for the rights of others.

The next day, I was surprised to hear Suzie say: "Burt thanks you for accepting the award. When I gave it to him, he said, 'Wow, it weighs a ton.' "

I was shocked — that was not the picture I was getting from Eric Monte. When I recounted the story to him, he looked at me wide-eyed. "I can't believe that," he said.

I finally put it together. Burt and Suzie had been married for only about two months when Burt was struck down. What kept her going now was her optimistic attitude. Whenever I talked with her, she always made it seem as if the next day Burt would be walking out of the apartment. She needed that optimism to function.

October 20, 1994. I was up in Fillmore again. I so vividly remember looking across the valley at that mountain that had split. Wind and rain had not yet had time to soften its raw wound. The phone rang.

It was my son Joel calling from Cedars-Sinai Medical Center, where he was recuperating from a hip replacement and watching CNN nonstop to pass the time. He had heard the announcement come over the news. My world shook as violently as it had when the earthquake hit. Burt was dead.

Burt and I used to joke about who would do the eulogy for the other. It seemed funny at the time, when death felt so far away. He always said, "Don't worry. When I give your eulogy, I'll lie like hell. You'll go off smelling like a rose."

He had a sense of humor about all things, especially what was most serious. I'll never forget that laugh of his — "Ha, ha, ha" — which the comics often imitated.

He called me Koik and I called him Boit. That

started years ago, when I went to Brooklyn to watch the Dodgers play. As I walked to my seat, a fan yelled out: "Hey Koik, how's Boit?" Burt found that very funny, and the nicknames stuck.

When you are young, you don't realize the importance of a good friend. But when death is peering over your shoulder, you begin to think about things that count. Often it's too late. Oh, Boit, I thought, Koik will miss you.

We had been friends for nearly fifty years. We started out in Hollywood at the same time — 1946. I had done *The Strange Love of Martha Ivers*, and Burt made a big hit in *The Killers*. Our first film together was *I Walk Alone* for producer Hal Wallis.

I had a five-picture deal with three to go, but Wallis insisted on changing it to a term contract — that meant being a slave to him for seven years.

Of course at that time every working actor was signed to a studio or an independent producer like Hal Wallis. Doing it on your own was tough. But seven years! That made me nervous, especially not knowing what movies he had planned for me.

I said, "Hal, tell me what you have in mind."

This made him very angry. "Look!" he snapped. "You're just a beginner. You'll do what I tell you to do. You sign, or I'll drop you."

I listened to a voice deep inside me and I obeyed it. "The hell with you," I said. "Drop me."

And he did.

Burt was still under contract to Wallis when I went off and made *Champion*, the movie my agents argued with me not to make. But again, I listened to that voice. *Champion* made me a star and earned me my first Academy Award nomination.

Then Hal Wallis swallowed his pride and came back to me. He formally submitted the script of *Gunfight at the O.K. Corral.* While I was reading it, Burt phoned. "If you play Doc Holliday, I'll play Wyatt Earp. And that will get me the fuck out of this contract."

For that movie, Burt received his final payment of $90,000. As a freelancer, I was paid $300,000. Oh, how Hal hated paying me that salary. That was a lot of money forty years ago.

The making of *Gunfight at the O.K. Corral* really cemented the friendship between Burt and me.

I will never forget one particular day on the set. We were filming a scene in which Burt is trapped in a saloon without a weapon, facing a gang of tough guys. I strut in and draw on them. With lightning speed I grab a gun out of one of the cowboy's holsters, toss it to Burt and the two of us dispose of about thirty thugs. Then we saunter out on the porch and Burt says, "Thanks." I was supposed to say, "Forget it," but the words never came out.

The ridiculousness of the situation struck us so funny that every time we got to that point in the scene, we would burst out laughing. We did it over and over again for hours. It was now nine o'clock at night. Wallis was furious. "Try it again!" But we never could make it. We would just bust out laughing. They finally had to stop the shooting, and we did it the next day.

Working with Burt was never dull. We argued a

lot. Some people thought that at times we would come to blows. But we never lost our sense of humor.

On location in Tucson, we would talk for hours after the shooting was over. Hal Wallis came up to me once and asked, "What do you guys find to talk about all that time?" He didn't realize that, between friends, talk is endless.

Yet there are still so many things we never covered, so many things I would like to talk about with my friend Boit.

After *Gunfight*, we were both pretty well established. And right around the same time, we started our own independent production companies, which was unheard of for an actor to do. Burt worked for my company in *Seven Days in May*, and I worked for his in *The Devil's Disciple*.

And as I look back, I realize that both of us were reaching out to try to do more than just action pictures or westerns. *The Devil's Disciple*, a play by George Bernard Shaw, would never have been made into a movie if the two of us didn't take cuts in our salaries to get it done. But we wanted to do something deeper, something worthwhile.

I fought to make *Paths of Glory* and *Lonely Are the Brave*, and failed to put together *One Flew over the Cuckoo's Nest*. He did *Birdman of Alcatraz*, a wonderful, sensitive portrayal, and other fine films — like *The Leopard* and *Judgment at Nuremberg*.

All through the years we ribbed each other.

When I was getting an award from the American Academy of Dramatic Arts, Burt was officiating. In eloquent style, he started off, "Kirk Douglas would be the first to admit that he is a very difficult man to work with." He took a pause and added, "And I would be the second."

I laughed. But then again, maybe he wasn't joking!

Our children grew up together.

Burt had five children; I had four.

His son Billy, who died at forty-nine, had been a great buddy of my son Joel. When I was shooting *Lonely Are the Brave*, I made plans to have lunch with Joel, who was then fourteen, at the studio. Since I only had an hour break, I was anxious for him to be on time. We made the date for noon but Joel didn't arrive until almost one o'clock, mumbling that he had been visiting with his friend Billy at Burt's house.

I was angry — I had waited all that time and now I had to get back to the set. As I was reprimanding Joel for being late, he put up his fists in an aggressive pose. I was shocked. "What are you doing, raising your hand against your father?!"

Shamefaced, Joel stuttered, "Well, Mr. Lancaster said, if you complain . . . I should stand up to you."

When I saw Burt next, I asked him about it, but he only laughed. "Ha, ha, ha . . ."

We did so many things besides making movies. A play, charity appearances, song-and-dance routines for special occasions.

When Burt and I were shooting *The Devil's Disciple* in London, we took part in a charity per-

132

formance at the Palladium. We spent hours working out a song-and-dance routine. We were excited about it, but when we arrived backstage on the night of the performance, we panicked. The audience was a bunch of upper-crust British stuffed shirts. Such comedy greats as Sid Caesar and Imogene Coca went on and hardly got a laugh. Then Sir Laurence Olivier did a comedy skit to just a few chuckles. We looked at each other: "They're going to kill us!"

Our music cue started, and we came on dressed in cutaways, doffed our bowler hats, bowed and walked to the footlights. Thunderous applause. We were

Boit and Koik were smash at
the London Palladium.

startled, but we broke into the song we had rehearsed so many times, trying for a cockney accent: "Maybe it's because I'm a Londoner, that I love London so . . ." More applause.

Then we went into a soft-shoe dance that ended with me climbing up on Burt's shoulders and waving to the crowd as we sang the last refrain. At the end, we tumbled to the floor and somersaulted off stage. The response was tumultuous. We couldn't believe it!

Drunk with our success, we worked out a similar routine for Academy Awards night, singing, "It's great not to be nominated . . ." Of course, that was before Burt broke up our act by winning an Oscar for *Elmer Gantry*.

Burt made the acrobatics look easy. He was a natural athlete who started his career in the circus, with his pal Nick Cravat. They had a routine using a twenty-foot pole. Little Nick, five foot seven, would hold the pole and big Burt, six foot two, would climb up and do stunts on top.

Of course Nick was his best friend. Burt trusted him with his life. Do you know what it means to be balancing a twenty-foot pole with your best friend on top of it? If you slip or fall, it's over.

During Burt's illness, Suzie tried to cut down Nick's visits because he would just come up there and sob. Nick died a few months before Burt.

Perhaps because of his circus background, Burt didn't take the art of acting too seriously. He was a natural, and he had very little patience with the students of Method acting.

We both agreed that the best example of the

Method school, the brilliant Marlon Brando, probably ruined hundreds of actors because so many tried to imitate his unique talents. Scratching your crotch is not enough.

We laughed at the childishness of our profession. Grown men pretending to be cowboys, staring each other down, eyes narrow slits, hands twirling guns loaded with blanks. But because we were both kids at heart, we enjoyed it.

Of course, there was a mature side to Burt. I often threatened to expose him to the world, to reveal him as the intellectual that he really was — a lover of literature and opera. He knew many arias by heart, humming them on the set. He cared deeply about social causes and he made me contribute to his American Civil Liberties Union activities because he so strongly believed in guarding the Bill of Rights.

But I'll let him go out a tough, macho guy. I'm too good a friend; I won't tell anybody about his gentler side.

Like all good friends, we passed through some rocky times, when our black moods got the best of us.

One day Burt called me, very excited. He had just read a two-character play, *Boys in Autumn*. It was based on the premise that Tom Sawyer and Huckleberry Finn meet again, not having seen each other for fifty years.

I found a lot of flaws in the script, but Burt's enthusiasm convinced me to give it a go.

Our rehearsals were a nightmare. We fought

every day about changes. At one time our argument became so heated, I decided to quit, and I walked off the stage. Burt followed, pleading with me. I turned to tell him off, and stopped — there were tears in his eyes. I had never seen Burt cry before. I couldn't believe that doing this play meant so much to him. That changed my mind.

Boys in Autumn opened in San Francisco and played for six weeks. We got standing ovations every night. But the price was too high.

For the first time, we realized that we were getting older. It was a two-character play. It was tough doing that every night plus two matinees. We were exhausted. We hadn't anticipated how much energy it would require from us — until then, energy was something we always had too much of.

Both of us were approaching seventy at the time. Up to then we were unstoppable, and our age in years meant nothing, but we were beginning to realize that no one escapes old age — it scared us.

Unanimously, without argument, we decided not to take the play to New York.

About that time, two young screenwriters, James Orr and James Cruickshank, were struck by the same idea — "Let's see these two old guys in a movie again" — and they wrote *Tough Guys* for us.

This time Burt was not so sure about the script, while I loved it. I had to twist his arm a little, but he finally agreed to do it. A shooting date was set, but we had to change it because Burt wanted to go to Europe. We set another date to accommodate his schedule.

Shortly after he came back, I got a call from Jeff Katzenberg at Disney Studios, upset about their investment — it seems Burt had notified them he had decided not to do the movie.

I got Burt on the phone. I was furious; I called him every dirty name I knew. I felt betrayed, but Burt couldn't see the tears in my eyes.

He reconsidered. The next week we started shooting the picture, and we had a good time doing it, joking around like the old days, although I could see that Burt's health was failing.

My God, is it over? Wasn't it just a few years ago that we were young actors starting our careers, looking up to veterans like Spencer Tracy and Humphrey Bogart?

Somebody must have been shuffling the cards too fast. But we have to play the hands that we're dealt.

Burt's stroke hit him about a year before I myself ended up in the hospital after my helicopter crash. At the time, I thought a lot about Burt. I felt sorry for him. He'd had two heart attacks, and now *this*. My God, I thought, it must be awful to have a stroke.

I remembered when, some years ago, I visited him at his home in Malibu. On the beach he showed off, doing a backward flip from a standstill. I was impressed. And then he said to me, "You know, when I can't do that I am going to quit the business."

Well, of course, when you can do a standing backward flip, you have the feeling that you can do it forever. You are young, and life seems eternal.

Burt stopped doing backward flips and still kept making movies, some of his best — *Atlantic City, Rocket Gibraltar, Field of Dreams.*

I had never seen *Field of Dreams,* but the day after he died, I went down to the video store and rented it. It was a fascinating film. Burt played a small role, but he was so effective. He appeared on the screen walking down the street; in his seventies he still had that erect, graceful, athletic walk. The camera came in closer — as he talked he used his hands in his characteristic elegant way. All those mannerisms were so familiar to me. I used to imitate them for the amusement of the movie crews: his walk, his laugh — "Ha, ha, ha" — with the teeth showing. He did the same to me, exaggerating my clenched jaw and bowlegged stroll.

When the tape went to black I realized that Burt is not dead; he will never die. Kids who are not born yet will someday watch him swinging from the yardarm of a pirate ship, walking majestically down the streets of Tombstone, rushing into danger to right a wrong . . .

But our time together was so short, like videotape on fast forward. I want to hit the STOP button and start over.

Hey Boit! This is Koik . . . wait for me!

CHAPTER

FOURTEEN

When *Field of Dreams* was over, I stared at the blank screen for a long time. Was this Burt's last message to me? The movie had been quite different from what I had expected. It's all about obeying the voice inside you. A man hears a voice telling him, "Build it, and he will come." The man doesn't know what it means, but he obeys the voice — and magical things happen.

Often, I had heard a voice inside me telling me what to do. I wonder if Burt had had the same experience. I wish now that we had talked about such things, about spirituality, religion. I was surprised when he did the movie *Moses*. In that film the voice of God was the same as the voice of Moses, Burt's voice. It was the voice within. I wanted to ask him about that. In our endless conversations, there were still so many things we never got to talk about.

We all have a voice within us that speaks to us, guides us, but do we listen? In my life, I remember the times I did, and regret the times I didn't.

When I graduated from high school and desperately wanted to go to college, I didn't have enough money, so I went to work. After a year, a job came along that paid a hundred dollars a week — a very good salary back then. If I took it, I would be on easy street; I could buy a convertible and have my pick of girls.

But a little voice within said, No, don't take it. Go to college. Forget about a car. Hitchhike.

I did. It was hard, but going to college changed my life. Where would I be today had I taken that job?

A few years later, a graduate of St. Lawrence University, I was in New York getting started in my acting career. I had a chance to go on the road and play the juvenile lead in *Spring Again*. Wow, the juvenile lead! I could hear the applause as we traveled from city to city; I fantasized about a romance with the ingenue. But that little voice inside of me said, No, stay in New York. In New York I could play the walk-on in Guthrie McClintic's production of *The Three Sisters* with Katharine Cornell, Judith Anderson and Ruth Gordon.

It was the right decision, because in addition to being exposed to the most talented actors on the stage, this little part led to a much more significant role on Broadway, which led me to Hollywood.

This kind of thing happened to me over and over. Shortly after I came to Hollywood, my agent got me a costarring part with Gregory Peck, Ava Gardner and Ethel Barrymore in *The Great Sinner*; this was MGM's most important production of that year. But then someone brought me *Champion*, a powerful script being produced by a group of unknowns who had no money; I was drawn to this story of an antihero boxer who desperately tries to punch his way to self-esteem and dignity.

We talked endlessly, but there were so many other things I still want to discuss with my old friend, Burt Lancaster. *(Photofest)*

Reading the script, I thought, What other actor can say the lines "I don't want to be a 'hey you' all my life. I want to hear people call me Mister"? That role was made for me — a chance to express the turbulent feelings inside me.

The little voice said, Do *Champion*. My agent thought I was crazy. But I did *Champion* anyway. It made me a star, got me my first Oscar nomination. (By the way, *The Great Sinner* was a flop.)

Looking back, I realize that if I had obeyed the urgings of agents, I would have been out of this business a long time ago. An agent, a manager, can't know what's right for your creative soul. For that, you have to listen to that voice within. It is the spiritual part of you; it is the subconscious part that is saying something important.

The little voice inside of me said, Buy *One Flew*

Over the Cuckoo's Nest. I bought the rights to the book, went to New York and did it as a play on Broadway. It was not a big success. When I came back, defeated after trying to keep the play running, I said to my wife, "I brought them a classic and they don't even know it."

For ten years, I tried to get someone to put up a comparatively small amount of money to make it as a movie. Well, I didn't succeed, but my son Michael did. He was able to do what I could not do. But that little voice inside me was right — it was destined to be a huge hit. It won five Oscars and kick-started Michael's producing career, which eventually led to his stardom as an actor.

But for ten years I didn't understand why my desire to make this movie was being thwarted. Why was God telling me no, over and over again? But when Michael went up there to pick up his Oscar, I knew the answer. God was laughing again. "Dummy, this one was for your son." Thank God for unanswered prayers.

I wish that I had played the part of McMurphy but I have to admit now that I would have done it differently and probably not won the Oscar that Jack Nicholson deserved for his portrayal.

What I say now has taken me many years to realize. It was a long, hard job of self-examination because I had so much resentment at not being a part of a project that was so special to me. Now I see that sometimes things happen the way a power beyond my control meant them to happen. It was ordained that Michael should produce that movie,

Michael should get an Oscar and that someone else should play the role that I coveted.

In *Field of Dreams*, the audience is led to believe that Burt Lancaster's character could have been a great baseball player. But something more important was in the cards for him that he couldn't see at that time. Had he become a famous baseball player, he would never have become the wonderful doctor who later saved so many lives.

You know, the little voices are always with us, around us, over us. Is it the voice of God, the call of the soul, the voice of a beloved one, the guidance of an angel? I don't know. But I know this voice has been with me all my life.

Of course, I have to admit that there were times when I heard the voice but didn't obey it.

Forty years ago — I don't know what got into me — I decided I wanted to do a TV series called *The Bible Speaks*. Can you imagine that? Here I am at the top of my career — one of the highest-paid leading men in Hollywood, a guy involved in steamy affairs with one sexy woman after another — and I decide to make a TV series about the Bible.

My idea was that the solution to every problem could be found in the Bible. For example, a man is in a hotel room contemplating committing suicide; by chance he sees the Gideon Bible on the table, picks it up. In it, he finds the answer to his problem. Where I got this idea, I don't know. Because I certainly never used the Bible to solve the problems in my life. I never even read it.

But something in the deep recesses of my subconscious was prodding me to do this show. I didn't have much time, so I shot the pilot over a weekend. It was never picked up by any network. No wonder. When I watch the old footage now, I am embarrassed. It's twenty minutes of close-ups of me chopping wood in the forest. There is no plot, no story, no other characters. Just me listening to a voice telling me a story from the Bible — the story that turned me away from Judaism when I was fourteen. The story of Abraham's sacrifice of Isaac. Obviously, I was meant to study that story, reexamine my misconceptions, pick up the Bible myself. The voice was saying, Dummy, read the Bible! But I never did.

The film ended up on the shelf, and I went on to other things. How differently my life would have turned out if only I had paid more attention to that little voice then.

I am convinced that there are voices speaking to us, but we don't always listen. Oh, I'm not going to say that it is the voice of God. But my friend Mike Abrums thinks so. He has been my physical instructor for thirty years. Lifting weights daily, I have had many discussions with him about God. One day he gave me a simple poem he had written. Here is an excerpt:

> *Have you ever had the voice of God*
> *Penetrate your thought like a lightning rod?*
> *Some think He spoke only to a few*
> *but He spoke to me and He'll speak to you.*

They talked to Him — the prophets of old
their troubles to Him they always told;
they asked for help and what did He do?
He spoke to them and He'll speak to you.

So child of God, please remember this,
talk to your God if things seem amiss
He will hear and He'll answer too
Yes, He really will speak to you.

I don't know that I share the deep conviction that Mike seems to feel, but I know that often there is something deep down in our subconscious that is struggling to break through, only we are so involved in our mundane activities that we don't hear it. I know now that that voice forty years ago was *not* telling me to make a TV series on the Bible when I knew nothing about the Bible. It was telling me it was time to *read* the Bible. And here I was trying to tell other people to do it.

So why didn't I hear it? I wasn't tuned in.

It still amazes me that we can take a little radio with a tiny battery in a closed room and tune it to different channels and hear different voices coming to us clearly through the window, through the walls, through closed doors. When the radio is turned off, where are those sounds, those vibrations? They are all around us just the same, but we don't hear them.

How often do voices speak to us when we are not tuned in? Maybe the voice of God is all around us and within us, but we are not on the right wavelength.

What other voices have I heard, but ignored? What other voices has my subconscious responded to?

Someone shocked me by pointing out to me that all my books — my autobiography and my three novels — seem to have the same theme. Each is about a man who is coming to terms with himself, who is looking back at who he was, who he is and wondering who he will become. And each man is a Jew.

In *The Ragman's Son*, I examined my life. I am surprised to hear people say that it's a very Jewish book. One reviewer said it was about "a man's painful struggle with his Jewishness." I didn't realize I was writing that.

When I read it now, I see it plainly. I see that no matter how far I ran away from my Jewishness, it was always there. Like my shadow, I could not lose it. Sometimes it was behind me, or to the side, or in front of me, but it was always there. Sometimes it was faint, often clearly etched, but always there. I tried to get rid of it, but like a sticky substance, it went from one hand to the other, no matter how hard I tried to wipe it away.

In *Dance with the Devil*, I tackled the story of a man denying his Jewish identity. I was never like Danny Dennison, but sometimes I might have come uncomfortably close. Once I said I was half-Jewish. I kept company with people who were anti-Semites. Like Danny Dennison, it was an issue that I had to resolve for myself sooner or later. I finally had to be able to say loudly and with pride, "I am a Jew."

And yet — would you believe it — I was surprised when my friends said my novel was too Jewish. On my second try, I made the same mistake.

The hero of my second novel, *The Gift*, is handicapped. He is in love with a rich heiress who never knew that her father was Jewish. And he himself is also a Jew, a descendant of Marranos. The Marranos were Jews who, around the time of the Inquisition, converted to Christianity on the surface, but who secretly continued to practice Judaism. I was astonished to learn recently that the most poignant Jewish prayer, *Kol Nidre*, which opens the Yom Kippur service on the High Holidays, owes its origins to the Marranos. *Kol Nidre* — meaning "All Vows" — is a nullification of all vows and promises made throughout the year. I always thought it was an odd way to begin a service that asks for one's reinstatement in God's good graces. But *Kol Nidre* really refers to the vows the Marranos made to Christianity. On Yom Kippur they annulled those vows and begged God's forgiveness for betraying Judaism.

In *The Gift* I tried to create an exciting story that said some meaningful things — like the idea that big business should have a conscience. I wrote about the exploitation of the Mexicans in Nogales, one example of how we abuse so many underprivileged people in so many parts of the world. I wrote about the problems of abused and abandoned animals. I also tried to deal with the relationship of a father and son — a relationship that is so difficult to realize fully. I was just finishing that novel when the helicopter accident happened.

The questions that arose as a result of the accident had many reverberations, which found their way into my third novel.

For the first time in my life — even though I was in my seventies — I thought about death. Maybe someone was telling me that I had put those thoughts off long enough. We are all so afraid of death. We cling to the conceit that we might never die. We never understand what people like Albert Schweitzer mean when they say you can't really live life until you are aware of death, until it is a part of you, perched on your shoulder.

I finally realized that, but I arrived there kicking and screaming.

And so, it was inevitable that I should write a novel that dealt with death. As an actor I find it easier to deal with an important subject by first approaching it as make-believe. So in *Last Tango in Brooklyn*, I tried to deal not only with the inevitability of death, but also with the unpredictability of its arrival.

I remember a small dinner party some time ago when Irving Lazar, my literary agent, was telling my wife and me how well he had planned in his will for his wife, Mary, who was considerably younger than he. But Mary died first.

Never try to outguess that guy with the scythe in his hand. This is what I tried to deal with in my story about Ben (a guy like me, a Jew of course), who is in love with a much younger woman, Ellen (an Italian Catholic). Ben has to come to terms with his old age when he is in a helicopter crash. He breaks off with Ellen. Just when he gets over his insecurities — and puts his domineering daughter, who wants to mother him to death, in her place — he finds out that Ellen has a terminal illness.

That's how *Last Tango in Brooklyn* takes on the biggie — mortality — by pointing out how little control we have over our lives. How in the end we must submit to God. Where it leaves off is where this book comes in. This one is — finally — the telling of my personal struggle with God.

In the beginning of this book, I asked the questions *Why was I spared? Why am I still alive?* And here in chapter 14, I still don't have the answer. But I think that one reason I was spared was because I had not yet come to terms with my Judaism. I had never really come to grips with what it means to be a Jew.

My accident didn't bring about a new religious philosophy. Rather, it released deep feelings and emotions that were always there, held back by a lack of confidence in myself.

Sometimes I feel myself gasping because I am not following *Halakhah*, the Jewish path. And at other times, I feel myself gasping because I am racing down that path. I feel that I am out of breath and suddenly I think, How the hell did I get into this mess?

A part of me is saying, Wait a minute, you are

becoming too Jewish. Stop! And then another part of me kicks in, saying, Don't be afraid. Keep going, keep going.

At this point in my life, it's the second part that's stronger. I take a deep breath, and I keep going.

CHAPTER

FIFTEEN

So how did my road back begin?

Here's a shocker — with Jesus.

No, no, I am not a Jew for Jesus. I never believed, nor do I believe now, that he was the Messiah, or God in human form, or the son of God, not any more than we are all children of God. But, after Abraham, Moses and Einstein, he certainly was the most famous Jew that ever lived.

I have been fascinated with Jesus ever since I got beat up by big ol' Johnny who said I killed him. (Just shows you what Johnny was hearing at the dinner table.) I went running home to my mother with a bloody nose, protesting that I had done no such thing, and demanding to know who this Jesus was. But I got no answers from my mother or from my father.

I knew that Jesus had to do with the cross that was on top of all the churches in our town. I remember that my Catholic classmates always crossed themselves when they passed a church. But when I asked them questions about Jesus, they mumbled something about God or the son of God. So I was confused. Did they think that Jesus was a God or was he the son of God? Somehow he was supposed to be both. How was that possible? I suspected even they didn't know. They said it was one of those "divine mysteries."

At that point in my life I thought that all religions were screwy. Of course, I believed in God. To me God was an old man — a very, very old man. (Even older than I am now, but without a bad back.) God was a very fit and very powerful old man. I was sure of it. And if ever I ate ham or bacon, He would strike me down dead. One of my first shocking discoveries came when, trembling with fear, I bit into a ham sandwich and nothing happened to me. It tasted delicious, and I didn't even throw up. I thought He was probably busy with so many other things that He didn't notice.

I often wondered if my God was stronger than their God. But sometimes I thought that theirs must be stronger because I couldn't get a job delivering the *Evening Recorder* because I was a Jew.

Then I found out that Jesus was a Jew! Wow! Now that really perplexed me. People who hated Jews worshiped a Jew as a God? Then I found out that Jesus was not only a Jew, but a rabbi who gave sermons on the Torah.

Do Christians know that? I guess this is why M. Scott Peck in his *Further Along the Road Less Traveled* says that the gospels of Jesus are the best-kept secret of Christianity. So many people quoting Jesus have never read the gospels. Were they to read the gospels and maybe a little bit of the rest of the Bible they would realize that half the time Jesus is quoting Moses.

One of the most famous quotations attributed to

Jesus is: "You shall love the Lord your God with all your heart, with all your soul and with all your might. This is the greatest and the first commandment. And the second is like it. You shall love your neighbor as yourself."

The first sentence comes from Deuteronomy, the last from Leviticus, two of the Five Books of Moses, collectively known to Jews as the Torah.

I learned that the many ideas that Christianity later embraced as its own had in fact been introduced to the world by Judaism nearly two thousand years before Jesus. Ideas of love, compassion, kindness to strangers and the poor came from Abraham, the first monotheist, and were reiterated at Mount Sinai when the Torah was given a few hundred years later. The ideas of holiness of human purpose, reverence for life and self-discipline all come from the Torah.

I guess I shouldn't be surprised that the earliest followers of Jesus were all Jews. The Last Supper was the Passover seder, and the Holy Grail or chalice was a *Kiddush* cup, which every good Jew uses not only on Passover but on every Sabbath.

I learned that "Christ" was not his last name, but Greek for "Messiah," a word by which Paul, a Hellenized Jew, called him many years after his death. Paul was an interesting guy — a brilliant PR man who created the religion of Christianity. Before he came along, the followers of Jesus were a sect within Judaism called Nazarenes. Paul — whose real name was Saul of Tarsus — never met Jesus. Can you believe that? But Paul became the chief interpreter of Jesus' teachings, even eclipsing the chief apostle, Peter. It was through Paul's influence that the early Christians discarded the Law of the Torah, like the commandment of circumcision. It didn't take Paul long to find out that adult males don't like men wielding knives near their most vulnerable organs. While he was at it, he also dropped keeping kosher and not working on the Sabbath, and added a number of pagan rituals to their observance.

The Jewish objections to these "changes" were loud and clear. Back then — as now — the rabbis made it crystal clear that believing in Jesus as God, the son of God, or the Messiah was completely incompatible with the most basic tenets of Judaism. And that's when Paul turned on the Jews and began to pander to the anti-Semitism of the Greco-Roman world.

I wondered what Jesus would have said about all that. I started to read.

I was surprised to find in a growing number of books by Christian authors that the writers routinely questioned the accuracy of the statements attributed to Jesus in the gospels. *Jesus: A Life* by A. N. Wilson (my personal favorite), *The Gospel According to Jesus* by Stephen Mitchell and the works of the world-famous Jesus Seminar are just a few of more than a dozen out there. The so-called New Testament had been written fifty to one hundred years after the death of Jesus. Could it be that the gospel writers were more influenced by Paul than by Jesus? Could it be that they elaborated on what Jesus had said?

Then I heard about *The Jefferson Bible* — on C-Span, of all places. They were covering President-elect Clinton's bus trip from Arkansas to the White House, and he made a pit stop at Monticello, Thomas Jefferson's home. Showing Clinton around, the guide pulled out the original copy of a personal Bible that Jefferson had compiled and which he called *The Life and Morals of Jesus of Nazareth.* Jefferson had excised all the lines from the four gospels that he did not believe Jesus had said. He left in what he considered "the diamonds" of authentic wisdom. The rest he called "vulgar ignorance," pronouncing it "impossible that such contradictions should have proceeded from the same being." No wonder that Jefferson was called an atheist for his revolutionary beliefs about Christianity.

But his small "Bible" survived. It is still handed to each member of the U.S. Senate when he or she is sworn in. I bought a copy and read it. Wow, Jesus sure had a temper. He threw out the money changers from the Temple. If he walked the earth today, what would he do if he entered the Vatican and looked around at such opulence, while so many people are starving?

So many things Jesus said made more sense in the context of Judaism than Christianity. Take the Lord's Prayer, Jesus's famous address to God:

•*Our Father who art in Heaven, Blessed be Thy name . . .* Hundreds of Jewish prayers start exactly like that.

• *Forgive us our trespasses, just as we forgive those who trespass against us*. It is the Jewish idea that God forgives trespasses against God, but people must ask and grant each other forgiveness. Yet this is an idea counter to the Catholic notion of a confessional where a priest, on behalf of God, absolves you from any and all sins you might have committed, whether against God or people.

• *Lead us not into temptation* . . . Why would God lead man into temptation? Don't Christians believe that this is Satan's domain, that Satan alone is responsible for the evil in this world? But it's a Jewish idea that God created absolutely everything — good and bad, angels and devils. It is Satan's job, *acting on God's behalf*, to test people so that they can make their own choices. Otherwise there would be no free will. Judaism says that when the human being withstands temptation Satan dances with joy; but when a human being falls prey to temptation and does an evil act, Satan weeps because he has done his job too well.

This Jesus sounded more and more Jewish to me, and definitely at odds with modern Christianity. Furthermore, there was no valid evidence that he ever claimed to be the son of God (indeed, he pointedly called himself "son of Man") and none whatsoever that he ever claimed to be God Himself.

What would he have said about anti-Semitism? What does he think about the millions and millions of people who have been murdered in his name? What would he have said about the Crusades, the

Inquisition, the Holocaust? The Nazis who so brutally exterminated six million Jews considered themselves Christians. The Pope never spoke out publicly against the Nazis. Apologists now say that he was trying to stay neutral and protect the Vatican. But in those days the Vatican also preached that Jews killed Jesus.

It is true that some Jews denounced Jesus, but it was the Romans who crucified him — the gospels themselves say so. And yet the Catholic Church uses Latin, the language of the Roman Empire, as its sacred tongue for religious services and religious pronouncements of any import. Explain that to me, would you?

The Christians, who conveniently condemned Jews as "Christ killers" while absolving the Romans, also preferred to think of him as a blond-haired, blue-eyed Aryan type rather than the swarthy, probably quite dark, Semite that he was.

I wondered if there was any reliable information on what he really looked like, any portraits of him as a Jew.

It astounded me that my favorite artist, Chagall, who had made the lithographs of all the prophets on the wall over my bed, also painted Jesus several times. "The White Crucifixion" is a huge oil done by Chagall in 1938; it now hangs in the Art Institute of Chicago. It is a striking rendering of Jesus on the cross, partially covered by a *tallis*, a Jewish prayer shawl. Around him are painted vignettes of pogroms, synagogues burning, Jews fleeing from the Nazis. This Jewish portrait of persecuted Jesus and persecuted Jews was Chagall's response as an artist to what was happening then in Nazi Germany.

I bought a copy of the painting and hung it on the wall of my room beside the other Jewish biblical figures. I felt it should be there, because studying Jesus, the *man,* made me a better Jew.

Scenes from the lives of Jews as depicted by Chagall in 1938. (*Oil on canvas, 1938, 154.3 x 139.7 cm. Gift of Alfred S. Alshuler, 1946.925. Photograph © 1996 The Art Institute of Chicago. All Rights Reserved. © 1997 Artists Rights Society [ARS] New York/ADAGP, Paris)*

Of all the things I read of him, the one that influenced me the most was this speech of Jesus recorded by the gospel writer Matthew:

"Do not think that I have come to destroy the Law or the Prophets. I have not come to destroy, but to fulfill. Surely, I say to you, till heaven and earth pass away, not one jot or one tittle shall be lost from the Law till all things have been accomplished. Therefore whoever does away with one of these least commandments, and so teaches men, shall be called least in the kingdom of heaven; but whoever carries them out and teaches them, he shall be called great in the kingdom of heaven."

To my mind, Jesus said quite plainly that one must obey the Torah. I was embarrassed to admit that I knew next to nothing of the Torah. Oh, sure, I knew it was the first five books of the Bible — Genesis, Exodus, Leviticus, Numbers and Deuteronomy. I knew it contained the stories of Adam and Eve, Abraham, Isaac and Jacob, the exodus of the Jews from the slavery of Egypt and their wanderings in the desert for forty years. But beyond that I knew zip.

Why was the Torah so important to Jesus? What was the Law for Living that it supposedly communicated? These questions fascinated me. I had some more reading to do.

CHAPTER

SIXTEEN

While I was becoming fascinated with Jesus, my editor Ushi was becoming fascinated with Judaism. Out of the blue, in the fall of 1993, she announced that she was going to Israel. A whole month in Israel would cost her a mere $950, plane fare, food and lodging included. Could that be true? Oh yes, but she was doing it through an organization called Volunteers for Israel, which basically meant she was going into the Israeli Army for three weeks. I didn't believe her. But she did it. Spent three weeks in fatigues working on an army base, oiling tanks or something, but she saw all of Israel.

While she was there, I asked her to look around for a project my charitable foundation might get involved in concerning children. She came back and told me that what was sorely needed were playgrounds, particularly for the children of the newly arrived immigrants from Russia and Ethiopia. This idea appealed to me very much.

In a world where there are so many lobbyists for different causes it's hard to find an advocate for children. They cannot speak for themselves. I have often watched reports on CNN from war-torn countries, seen the tearstained faces of little children and wondered — do they have happy moments? Do they ever get to play? Where do they play among the bombs and mine fields? Even in a peaceful, overdeveloped country like America, capitalists discuss their problems on manicured golf courses while kids play in gutters.

When I was a kid in Amsterdam, New York, we didn't have playgrounds or parks for children. We played in the streets — the usual games, stickball, tag, though we had some "special events" that we saved for newcomers to the neighborhood. "House on fire" was one of these, a favorite. We'd instruct the victim to close his eyes and lean against the telegraph pole, count to ten and yell "house on fire." As he was counting, we'd circle him, unbutton our pants and get ready. When he yelled "house on fire," we'd put it out. Another favorite was "let 'er fly." We'd place our new neighbor on the opposite side of the street, his back to us, and tell him to count to ten, then turn around and yell "let 'er fly." As he was counting, we'd hurriedly pick up whatever was handy — manure, cans, any kind of trash available. When he turned around and yelled "let 'er fly," he was met with a bombardment of detritus. Kids sure were cruel then, but maybe a nice place to play off the streets would have made them kinder, if less inventive.

The houses on Eagle Street were close together, and a cacophony would emerge from all of them at once — immigrants from Russia, Poland, Italy, Ireland, Germany, all yelling in their native tongues. (In my house, it was Yiddish.) I learned a lot of expressions like *suki syn* (Russian for "son of

161

a bitch"), *fan'culo* (Italian for "up yours") and my favorite, *daj mi buzi* (Polish for "give me a kiss"). There was an overdeveloped blond Polish girl who often obliged.

When it was too noisy in the street (and at home it wasn't quiet with six sisters), I would run away to an empty field near the carpet mills. Lying down in the weeds beside a little pond, I'd listen to the sounds in the distance.

That field and other rural areas outside of town are gone now, replaced by housing developments and paved supermarket parking lots. I've always had a hard time going back to my hometown to see the one place of a few happy childhood memories slowly, but surely, disappearing.

I had made more than twenty films before my town finally noticed me. They decided to put my name on something, and someone was dispatched to ask me what would make me feel honored. I said, "Build a park for children."

And so they did.

With those nostalgic memories in my mind, I got the idea of building a park in Beverly Hills. There was an empty, ill-kempt lot near my house that belonged to the city. I offered to pay the full cost of making it into a beautiful park. I paid for a landscape design that alone cost $15,000; the estimate for the finished job was $350,000. I offered to put up all the money.

Then the bureaucracy kicked in.

You can't just *give* something to the city. You must have committee meetings, neighbors' hearings, approvals. Red tape. No matter how much you might be willing to pay, there has to be competitive bidding, a lengthy and complicated process.

In the end, frustrated by it all, I told them, "Let's make everybody happy — let's forget it."

It was the best thing that could have happened. Because it suddenly hit me — does Beverly Hills need another park? Does it need *more* trees and flowers? I must have been insane.

Instead, my wife came up with the idea of putting the money to better use by doing something to improve the pathetic condition of school playgrounds in poor sections of Los Angeles. Most of them are deplorable because there are no funds to improve or maintain them. So now we have committed one million dollars from our foundation for that purpose. Children must have a place to play and get off the street.

And while I was at it, I started building parks in Israel too.

So far, the one I am most proud of is the playground for little Arab children in the densely packed slum called the Moslem Quarter inside the walls of the Old City of Jerusalem.

The poorest of the poor live here — some twenty-five thousand souls. Many of the Arab homes used to belong to Jews, as testify the small diagonal hollows in the stone doorways, where once rested *mezuzahs,* the little scrolls with a piece of text from the Torah: *"You shall love the Lord your God with all your heart, with all your soul and with all your might . . ."* The original residents of those houses had fled or were murdered in 1948, when the Arabs refused to acknowledge the United Nations resolution creating the state of Israel and drove the Jews out of the Old City. Since the 1967 Six Day War, when Jews once again gained access to this ancient fortress, they have tried to purchase those homes from the Arabs. As poor as they are, the Arabs are afraid to sell, certain that they will be killed by terrorists for selling to Jews.

So the powerless poor remain perpetual victims. You walk through the narrow, stench-filled alleys and see small children pulling the heavy wagons of the street vendors. How many of them get to finish school? How many have a chance to play?

There was an open area, where an old British Army compound used to be, surrounded by old trees. The kids used the dirt lot to kick around a soccer ball. I wanted to make it into a real playground. With Mayor Ehud Olmert's enthusiastic permission, I went ahead.

I couldn't imagine why the oil-rich Arab brethren of the Palestinians couldn't have done something like that here a long time ago. The cost was much less than a sheikh's evening out on the town. A couple of years ago, I was invited to a lavish Hollywood dinner feting a Saudi prince interested in investing in movies. During the meal, he took a liking to Goldie Hawn — undoubtedly ignorant of the fact that this blond-haired bombshell is Jewish — and gave her his worry beads. All perfect rubies. That little trinket would have built a few playgrounds. (She politely gave them back to him.)

The Israeli Arab who runs social programs for the poor of the Old City was very grateful for my gift and apologetic about his wealthy Arab neighbors. He had no explanation for their lack of concern, but he volunteered, "I am convinced that the Jews give most of the charity in the world. It must be a cultural difference."

Jews *do* give. American Jews, for example, though representing only two percent of the U.S. population, have made the United Jewish Appeal the second-largest charity in America, and it is only one of many charitable organizations that depend on Jewish support.

Just the other day I read in the *Los Angeles Times* about a man who gave $500 million to help legal immigrants in this country. Before I even started reading the article, I wondered if he was a Jew. (He was.) Why do Jews give? It's in their genes. The Talmud says that giving to others is not charity, it's justice. You must do it. Even a beggar must give to another beggar who has less. Someone always has less than you. The Jews today who are big philanthropists may not know why they are giving. It's like those people in Arizona and New Mexico who go down to the cellar to light candles every Friday night. They don't know why; it's just a family custom. They don't know that their ancestors were Marranos, Jews who pretended to be Christians but who secretly observed the Jewish rituals of the Sabbath.

At the entrance to the playground in the Moslem Quarter I had them make a sign — IN MEMORY OF

A Douglas Playground in the heart of the Old City,
Jerusalem, for Arab children.
(© *Brian Hendler Photography*)

The dedication of the
Douglas Playground
in Talpiot, Jerusalem.
Mayor Ehud Olmert
is looking on.
(© *Brian Hendler
Photography*)

THE OKLAHOMA CHILDREN — for those poor, innocent children who died when a terrorist set off a bomb at the Oklahoma City Federal building. It seemed to me fitting to dedicate a playground in their memory in the Holy City of Jerusalem, where children are no strangers to terrorists' bombs.

Not long after the park was completed, Hamas started a new offensive against Israel. I watched the horrible aftermath — the bloody bodies of little children strewn on the sidewalk. I decided to continue building parks and playgrounds in Israel. I am now up to five, and someday I hope to make it ten.

When the first playground was ready, I went to Israel for the dedication. This was back in September of 1994.

After the ceremonies my old friend Teddy Kollek, the former mayor of Jerusalem, along with the staff of the Jerusalem Foundation, gave me a tour of the city. They showed me the newly erected soccer field, the biggest supermarket in Jerusalem and the new zoo. I understand that secular Israelis yearn to re-create an American lifestyle for themselves, and that a supermarket was a step in that direction, but frankly if I wanted to see a spectacular supermarket, I could have stayed in Beverly Hills. And, to me, a zoo is a terrible waste of money. I'm against incarcerating animals. Why go to stare at poor miserable creatures in cement cages when you can see fantastic films of them behaving like the wild things they are in their natural environment?

That's not what I wanted to see in the Holy City. When people like me come to Jerusalem, they want to see and experience what *only* this ancient city has to offer. Something that no other city or country can duplicate. Something spiritual.

This is the center of the world's three most important religions — Judaism, Christianity and Islam. The very stones upon which began the spiritual odyssey for so many of the world's people are right here. The traditions that have been observed for four thousand years are still observed here. But many secular Israelis seem to be embarrassed by the spiritual side of Israel.

I felt unfulfilled as my wife and I made our way to the hotel, but there the reception touched me. Everyone seemed so glad to see me again, after a twelve-year absence. They ushered us into our

At the gravesite of Oskar Schindler in Jerusalem.

room, and I was amazed. They had put my initials — KD — on the towels, bathrobes, everything. I was moved and very flattered until Anne said, "Honey, this is the King David Hotel."

I walked to the window and stared out at the magnificent view of the Old City, its ancient fortress walls surrounded by grass and flowers.

I first saw that view more than forty years ago, when I came to Israel to make *The Juggler* — a movie about a Holocaust survivor who had lost his Jewishness and finds it again in Israel. But back then, when I looked out of the window of this same King David Hotel, where the grass and flowers now grow, I saw Arab soldiers pacing back and forth, making sure no Jew got close to the Old City. This was a painful time, when Jews were not even allowed to go cry at the Wailing Wall. No other invader of Jerusalem over the centuries had been that cruel.

How Israel had changed since then.

So many new things — the newest being the park I had built. But even though I had come for the dedication, that was not really what had brought me here. I knew where I had to go. I rushed out of the hotel.

The *Kotel* — the Holy Wall, the Wailing Wall — was bathed in the golden rays of the setting sun.

The Wall was once a part of the foundation of the Temple; it was destroyed by the Romans, who banished the Jews from their homeland, which they renamed Palestine after the Philistines, then the most vicious enemies of the Jews.

When I got there, the plaza beneath the Wall was crowded with worshipers. The energy emanating from all the praying Jews, *davening* at a wild pace, was overwhelming.

I thought of the story, often told, of a blind, poor and childless man who prayed daily at the Wall that his fate might be reversed. And one day, during his fervent prayer, he heard the voice of God: "I'll answer your prayers. I'll give you one thing. What do you want most?" The man was thrown into an emotional frenzy. What should he ask for? If he asked for sight, seeing his poverty would only bring him grief. If he asked for wealth, what good would it be if he was still blind and had no children with whom to share his good fortune? But if he asked for children, how, being so poor, could he feed them? Besides, it would break his heart not to be able to see them. Thus he agonized, and finally he formulated this prayer: "Dear God, grant me just one thing — the joy of seeing my children eating off of gold plates."

Only a Jew would come up with a prayer like that!

I moved through the crowd. It was difficult to find a place to touch the Wall. I looked around for a crevice where I could put the tiny, folded-up piece of paper with my prayer. I found one. As I reached deep into it, my fingers touched other pieces placed there before mine. I hoped that all those prayers had been answered.

As I extricated myself from the *davening* throngs, I thought how much more frenzy there would be here tomorrow evening — Friday — when the worshipers gather here to welcome the Sabbath.

The Sabbath — *Shabbat* — is an ancient Jewish custom celebrating the day when God, having created the world, rested. It is the Fourth of the Ten Commandments: *"Remember the Sabbath day and keep it holy."*

Many Jewish thinkers have seen the observance of the Sabbath as the key to the survival of the Jewish people — a means of recharging the spirit in the face of insurmountable odds and relentless persecution. It's been said: "More than the Jewish people have kept the Sabbath, the Sabbath has kept the Jewish people."

I wanted to have that holy experience in this holy city.

Ushi, who, after her experience in the Israeli army, had come back again for a period of study, had told me about a fascinating young rabbi in Jerusalem — Rabbi David Aaron. He had played in a rock band and wanted to make a career as a musician until he made his first visit to Israel, bumped up against Judaism and became a rabbi instead. He eventually established a school in Jerusalem called Isralight Institute, where adults come to discover what they never had learned as children — "the joy of Judaism." That sounded like an oxymoron to me. I was curious. I called the rabbi and made a date to have Shabbat dinner at his house.

The day before Shabbat, Anne and I were honored by an invitation to a lunch at the modest apartment of Prime Minister Yitzhak Rabin. His apartment was on the top floor of a simple apartment building near Tel Aviv. We went up in a small elevator, and there was one soldier standing in the hall by his door. The meal for about a dozen people was prepared by Leah, the prime minister's wife. How different from having lunch at the White House.

At the end of the luncheon they invited us to a big dinner in Tel Aviv on Friday night. I declined, because I wanted to be in Jerusalem for Shabbat. Rabin raised his eyebrows but said nothing. As we were walking out, he took Anne aside and whispered, "Don't let him get too involved."

His reaction astounded me. What was wrong with having a spiritual experience? Did he think that the rabbi would get me to grow *payes*, wear

With Prime Minister of Israel Yitzhak Rabin, a year before his assassination.

tzitzit and a *kippah?*

But during my stay in Israel, I came to realize that many Israelis were not Jewish enough. They had become so secular that many were losing the significance of the spiritual element. Even in secular America, the president goes to church every Sunday, but before Bibi Netanyahu, the Israeli prime ministers never went to the Wall to acknowledge a Higher Authority. During the signing of the peace accords I noted that King Hussein of Jordan quoted from the Bible; Rabin did not. Such is the schism between religious and secular Jews in Israel that some of the secular actually disdain the Torah.

Another tragedy is that even though there are many factions among the religious sects of Israel, the secular Israelis prefer to lump all religious people — good and bad — into one fanatical pot they can readily dismiss. It's true that those few with a dangerous, holier-than-anyone attitude are the worst and give all Jews a bad name, but they are a tiny minority that gets a lot of press. The mainstream religious would do well to be more vocal in disavowing the more radical and fanatical fringe element among them.

A year after my meeting with him, Rabin was assassinated. A Jewish religious fanatic murdered a Jewish leader who had served the people of Israel in four wars and was now trying to establish a lasting peace. Most religious Jews, just as secular Jews, mourned the loss of their leader.

One of the most poignant messages I received

after Rabin's assassination was from Rabbi Aaron:

> Today I am ashamed to be a Jew . . . When a gentile kills a Jew, it is murder. When a Jew kills a Jew, it is suicide.
>
> This horrifying crime is not just the act of some madman. It is the culmination of the tragic polarization of our people. A bitter war of mutual disrespect and insult has been raging for years . . .

He was brokenhearted, and his words broke my heart too.

But I am getting ahead of the story. Because at the time of my lunch with Rabin, I had not yet met Rabbi Aaron. That was to happen the next day.

We met by the Zion Gate and walked through the Jewish Quarter.

I said, "Look, Rabbi, I want you to know that I am not much of a Jew. Judaism lost me at age fourteen."

What he said in response staggered me. He pointed out that no rational adult would make a business decision based on what he knew when he was fourteen. No one would decide whom to marry based on what he knew about love and relationships when he was fourteen. But lots of people seem satisfied to dismiss religion based on what they learned — or didn't learn — at fourteen.

He was right, and I was one of those that stupid.

I was stuck back at age fourteen, staring at a picture in my Hebrew book — Abraham with his long beard bent over a frightened little boy, in his hand a long knife. That boy looked a lot like me. Okay, so Isaac didn't die, but he came close. I bet he didn't go for a walk with his father after that. Tell *him* that it was only a test from God.

That's what I was remembering as Rabbi Aaron took us up to the rooftop of his school. He kept talking in a low voice as the sun continued to sink. The rays bounced off the gold of the Dome of the Rock, the icon of Islam dominating this ancient Jewish city.

It's fascinating how it came to be built there. Some six hundred years after Jesus, a man named Mohammed from Mecca, a city in what is now Saudi Arabia, had a revelation from God that the Arabs were descendants of Abraham's son Ishmael. He studied the Torah, adopted many of its laws, and pronounced his love for his Jewish brethren — all dutifully recorded in the Koran. But he also demanded that the Jews recognize him as a prophet. When they ridiculed his claim, he responded with fury, and turned on the Jews with a vengeance. He also turned on the Christians. (Ironically, it was the Moslem persecution of the Christians that saved the Jews, who were then in danger of annihilation by the Byzantine Church.) When Mohammed died in Medina, also in Saudi Arabia, his followers announced that he was mystically transported to Jerusalem for his ascent to heaven, and they built the beautiful Dome of the Rock to mark the site.

As my eyes traveled around the Old City, the rabbi pointed out the Moslem Quarter, the

175

Christian Quarter, the Armenian Quarter and the Jewish Quarter. I could feel the holiness of the city, so important to so many. All these religions were rubbing shoulders with one another and hating the friction created by such closeness.

Yet it all began with one man — Abraham, the first monotheist. The three religions that now make their home here all claim him as father. They are all based on the Torah. Jesus studied Torah; Mohammed studied Torah. But I had never studied Torah. It was about time. And it was there — as the candles of Jerusalem were lit like stars — that I made a vow to do it.

As we left the rooftop, I kept thinking: I have been a Jew for over seventy years and I know so little about Judaism. Why am I still a Jew? I pushed those thoughts out of my head as we walked through the dark alleys to the rabbi's home.

I met his young wife, a former parachutist in the Israeli army, and his five children.

We ate a delicious meal and sang songs with the rabbi beating time on the table. Through the window I could see other houses lit by the warm light of candles and could hear the same songs echoing in the night. They were happy songs. I felt good.

That night I felt that I had come home. The light of the Shabbat candles transported me back seventy years. I could see my mother's face as she lit them each Friday night. I could hear her voice, just before she died: "What day is it?"

"Friday, Mama."

"Don't forget to light the candles . . ."

I made plans to start studying the Torah with the young rabbi the next time he came to America.

He told me that, in English translation, there are only 350 pages in the Torah. Not so many. I thought if God is a patient God, maybe he'll give me enough time to learn the things I need to know to understand this book that has made Jews the conscience of the world. Maybe I will understand why people hate us.

The next day, I took a tour through the tunnel along the foundations of the Temple. Archeologists had dug this tunnel, barely wider than a sewer pipe, to expose the entire Western Wall.

This is the same tunnel that was used as an excuse by Arafat to stage a series of riots against the new hard-line government of Israel. Arafat said the tunnel was going to undermine the mosque on top of the Temple Mount. Trust me, I was there: The tunnel goes nowhere near the mosque. It couldn't. The rocks of the wall are mammoth. One weighs 570 tons. Go dig through that.

The tunnel is as close as a Jew can get to the majesty and holiness of the Temple originally built by King Solomon. You feel like a rat burrowing into the history of your ancestors buried by the debris of so many conquerors.

As I walked slowly, following my guide, Tova Saul, a young religious girl who came from Pittsburgh to settle here, I let my fingers caress the huge blocks of stone.

We came to an archway, cemented in by the

Arabs, where a door had once led to the top of the Temple Mount. This is how the High Priest entered the Holy of Holies. As Tova was reciting some interesting facts about the archway, suddenly all went black. And I mean pitch black. The electricity was out. I didn't know what to do. I could hear voices of people calling to each other as they groped for the exit. When the lights go out, Israelis always worry. Are the Arabs attacking again? Are Scud missiles flying? The tunnel had only one way out then, and it wasn't easy to leave the way you came.

I was standing in what, for a Jew, is the holiest spot on earth. I decided to recite the only prayer I still remembered in Hebrew: *"Shema Yisrael Adonai Elohainu Adonai Ehad."* Hear, O Israel: the Lord our God, the Lord is One!

The lights came back on. "You want to leave?" Tova asked, anxiously looking to see if the temporary blackout had frightened me.

"No," I said, "let's go on." We continued down the passageway until we came to the end.

"This is it," Tova said, pointing to an exposed piece of rough stone in front of us. The stone was no longer part of the smooth wall. This stone was something else.

"What is it?"

"This is the bedrock of Mount Moriah."

I looked at this black stone enshrouded with so much mystical meaning.

"You mean . . ."

She finished it for me. "Yes, this is the bedrock of

the mountain where Abraham took his son Isaac to be sacrificed."

The picture from my Hebrew-school book flashed into my mind. But, to my surprise, it no longer frightened me. I wasn't sure why. Something had happened to me here that I didn't quite understand.

It was very quiet in the tunnel, dimly lit, cool.

Tova's voice was barely above a whisper: "This is where it all started."

I couldn't speak. She was right.

This place represented the beginning of my doubts. And, at long last, the end of them.

Here in the dark tunnel, touching the rock of Mount Moriah, I grew up.

Three years after the helicopter crash, when God first rattled my complacency, I had come full circle. Little did I know that this was just the beginning.

CHAPTER

SEVENTEEN

When I was a kid in *cheder*, Hebrew school, I learned all the Hebrew prayers. Once I even chanted the Friday-evening service at the local synagogue. Of course, I didn't know the meaning of a single prayer that I was chanting. But the small Jewish community of Amsterdam was so proud of me that they decided to pay for my education at a rabbinical school. I was horrified. How could I tell them? I didn't want to be a rabbi. I wanted to be an actor.

And so I ran away from that world, but now I was back. And all charged up to study the Torah. Why had I taken so long? I was probably the oldest beginning student of Torah in the world.

Rabbi Joseph Telushkin of the Synagogue for the Performing Arts heard about my trip to Israel and invited me to give a talk on the subject on Shabbat. I agreed. I related my experiences in the Holy Land and my new insight — that were it not for the pious, black-hatted, bearded Jews with their long *payes*, who never gave up on the Torah no matter what the world was doing, I might not have a Torah to study today.

I was surprised by the overwhelming reaction. The speech was reprinted in several Jewish newspapers and magazines, and invitations to repeat it flowed in from everywhere. All of this attention scared me. I was just trying to find out for myself a little about the meaning of being a Jew. I didn't want to be SuperJew. I was confused.

I declined all invitations to speak, and I wavered in my resolution to study the Torah. I don't know why, but it too scared me. And then I would argue with myself: Kirk, you're a jerk. What scares you? Is it that ancient word "Torah"? Then think of it as the Five Books of Moses that were given to your ancestors when they wandered in the desert for forty years. I didn't convince myself, and I decided to postpone my studies.

But that week, Rabbi Aaron arrived in Los Angeles and I was stuck.

During the time he was here we studied the Torah four to five hours a day. We read the Torah in the English translation on one side of the page, and occasionally the rabbi would point out a word or phrase in Hebrew on the opposite side to explain a different nuance. Our talks were like the commercial for the Eveready battery rabbit — they went on and on and on. But they were never boring. When he left Los Angeles we weren't out of the Garden of Eden yet.

But I was excited. When I first began to study Torah, I had been prepared to be immersed in the gibberish of "thou couldst," "thou wouldst" and "forsooths"; instead I found riveting stories filled with adventure, fratricide, murder, incest, adultery. Now I understood why it was the best-seller of all time. When I expressed that to Rabbi Aaron, he smiled. "Of course, the Torah is life."

Often I was amazed at God's patience with the "stiff-necked" Jews. I had to admit I had many of those stiff-necked genes.

I was sorry to see each week of study zip by. I couldn't wait for the next time Rabbi Aaron could come.

My rabbi in Jerusalem, David Aaron, in front of the Wailing Wall.
(© *Tova Saul*)

Meanwhile, I was invited to give a talk to a film class at the University of Southern California. The students were anxious for advice on how to make it in show business. One young man asked me for surefire script suggestions. I said, "Study the Torah — all the best scripts are there. Whatever dramatic device you can dream up, God thought of it first."

Word got around about my new passion.

People began whispering, "You know, Kirk is studying the Torah."

"He is?"

"And with a rabbi from Jerusalem!"

"Gee, I didn't even know he was Jewish!"

At a dinner party, someone would inevitably come up to me and say in a confidential tone, "Kirk, I hear you're studying Torah." And then he'd lower his voice. "You know, I was bar mitzvahed."

Of course, some thought it was a joke. I was amazed at the different reactions, especially from Jews. One Jewish friend called and started to rib me about my new interest. But as the conversation went on, he confided that he said a prayer every night to God — a Christian prayer, he hastened to add.

"What's the prayer?"

"That famous one: *The Lord is my shepherd; I shall not want . . .*"

I started to laugh. He was reciting Psalm 23 written in Hebrew by King David about a thousand years before Christianity.

It's a tragedy. Jews don't know what they have. Some don't even know what the Torah is. Perhaps I should have said I was studying the Bible. The

Torah is the first five books of any Bible, even the Christian Bible.

Actually, the Christian Bible is made up of two big parts, the Old Testament (which is the entire Hebrew Bible, including the Torah, the history of the Jewish people and the writings of the Kings and Prophets) and the New Testament (which consists of the teachings of Jesus and the letters of his apostles). Did you know that the Jewish part of your average Christian Bible covers about twelve hundred pages and the Christian part of the Christian Bible covers only about three hundred pages? The teachings of the Torah and the Prophets are integral to the teachings of Jesus.

Rabbi Aaron finally led me out of the Garden of Eden, only to plunge me into the travails of man

My rabbi in Los Angeles, Nachum Braverman, with his wife, Emuna, and their nine children. God said, "Be fruitful and multiply." (© *Gina Ferazzi/The Los Angeles Times*)

now in possession of the knowledge of good and evil. It was exciting stuff, and waiting for Rabbi Aaron to fly in from Israel once every six weeks made me too impatient. So I found a local rabbi to study with from an organization known as Aish HaTorah (Fire of the Torah), whose mission is to teach Torah to secular Jews like me. My new teacher, Rabbi Nachum Braverman, came from a totally nonreligious family; he wasn't even bar mitzvahed. A visit to Israel changed him, and he eventually became an Orthodox rabbi.

The most important thing I learned from my studies is that all the greats of the Bible came from dysfunctional families. That made me happy. It was reassuring to find out that they, like us, all had problems that they had to overcome — none of them were perfect. But the reason they are in the Bible is precisely because, in spite of that, they did something meaningful in life.

One of my favorite stories was that of Joseph. Let me give you a short Torah lesson, according to Rabbi Kirk:

Genesis, chapter 37, verse 2: *At seventeen years of age, Joseph tended the flocks with his brothers as a helper to the sons of his father's wives, Bilah and Zilpah. Joseph brought bad reports of them to their father.*

What is that teaching us? That Joseph was a fink. Joseph was a little tattletale: "You know, Daddy, what my brothers did?"

Verse 3: *Israel loved Joseph best of all his sons for he was the child of his old age and he had made him a coat of many colors.*

Okay. How would you like to be Joseph's brother and find that your father made him this special coat of beautiful colors! You have to wear some damn skin of an animal or something. And there is little Joseph prancing around with his fancy-shmancy outfit!

Verse 4: *And when his brothers saw that their father loved him more than any of his brothers, they hated him so that they could not speak a friendly word to him.*

Anyone can understand that. That seems reasonable to me. If I was one of Joseph's brothers, I would have helped them get rid of him.

Verses 5–8: *Once Joseph had a dream which he told to his brothers and they hated him even more. This is what he told them: "Hear this dream which I have dreamed. There we were binding sheaves in a field when suddenly my sheaf stood up and remained upright. Then your sheaves gathered around and bowed low to my sheaf." His brothers answered, "Do you mean to reign over us? Do you mean to rule over us?" They hated him even more for his talk about his dreams.*

The Torah is the best script I have ever read.
(© *Jonathan Torgovnik*)

Can you blame them? I think God is playing jokes here. Okay, we know the dream is going to be fulfilled. Eventually, they will be bowing to Joseph. But, God, do You think that was fair to rub it into them?

Of course, it is perfectly fine for Joseph to have the dream, but Joseph didn't have to go bragging to his brothers. The lesson to Joseph was: Keep your mouth shut! Why make them feel bad?

Verses 9–10: *He dreamed another dream . . . When he told it to his father and brothers, his father berated him . . .*

It was about time for the old man to say something about this spoiled brat.

But it was too late as far as the brothers were concerned. They sold Joseph into slavery and ripped up his fancy coat. They told their father he had been eaten by wild animals.

The father was plunged into perpetual mourning, and the brothers were happy that they got even with their brother and their father.

I see so much humor, so much irony in the Bible. But what attracts me most is the fact that all these people had to overcome their faults and do something with their life. It's a message to all of us. You may do a lot of bad things, but you can overcome your past. That is the reassuring thing you learn from the Bible.

Because the story of Joseph doesn't end there. In slavery, the spoiled brat grows up, matures and turns into a fine person who later on becomes a model of forgiveness.

While in the home of his master Potiphar, Joseph, who by all accounts was extremely good-looking, attracts the eye of his master's wife. Mrs. Potiphar presses her attentions on the slave, but he won't give in because he refuses to betray his master. Furious at the rejection, Mrs. Potiphar accuses Joseph of rape.

Have we heard this story recently?

Sure have. That was the plot of the movie *Disclosure*, starring my son Michael. What I told those USC kids is absolutely true — the best scripts come from the Torah.

The brothers too become better people. And there comes a time when they are all reunited.

No person can read that story without getting caught up in the heartbreaking drama of Joseph hugging his brothers, declaring, "I am your brother Joseph — is my father Jacob still alive?" When they beg his forgiveness, he tells them that everything that had happened was part of God's plan. Now that the Israelites are in the middle of a famine, Joseph is in an important position in Egypt and able to save his people from starvation.

Joseph forgives his brothers, and through that act an amazing thing happens. Four sets of brothers have clashed in Genesis — Cain and Abel, Isaac and Ishmael, Jacob and Esau, and Joseph and his brothers — but now forgiveness changes the course of Jewish history: Brother no longer betrays brother, but there are many more betrayals.

Take the story of King David, who gave us such beautiful psalms. He was quite a guy. One night, walking along the parapet on the roof of his palace, King David spied a beautiful naked woman bathing

— Bathsheba, who was married to one of his officers, presently away in battle. He sent for her and they made love that night. When she became pregnant, he ordered her husband sent to the front lines, and, as planned, the husband was killed. King David then married Bathsheba.

That's when the prophet Nathan paid a call on the king to tell him about a terrible wrong that had been committed in his kingdom — a man who had many sheep stole from a man who had only one, and then had him killed.

Incensed at the grave injustice, King David ordered the man put to death. "That man is you," said the prophet.

King David then saw the wrong that he had done and pleaded with God to grant him forgiveness. Shortly thereafter Bathsheba gave birth to the child of their illicit relationship, and the child died. King David mourned the death of his son, but he understood that this was atonement for his sins. King David was sincerely sorry, and God subsequently showed His favor by giving him another son — Solomon — who became the greatest king of the Jewish people.

God is a forgiving God. There is hope for me yet.

I can't tell you how much I loved learning these biblical stories. And I would repeat them to anyone who would listen.

One of those whose ear I so frequently bent was listening more closely than I thought — my son Michael.

CHAPTER
EIGHTEEN

My two wives were not Jewish and therefore, by Talmudic law, my sons are not Jewish either. When they were growing up, I did not hide my origins from them, but I did not give them any education in Judaism either. When asked about religion, my answer was that I did not want to impose any creed on my children; they could make their own choice when they were adults. Perhaps, inwardly, I hesitated to give them the burden of being a Jew, but, in truth, it was just a cop-out. I couldn't have fulfilled the commandment to teach the Torah diligently to my children, because I didn't know it myself. And what was worse, I didn't care about it then.

When I started to study Torah my kids didn't know how to react. At first they seemed a little bit amused, perhaps curious. I suspected that they nudged each other while rolling their eyes.

Then came the first shock. When visiting my son Peter around Hanukkah time, I found him lighting the menorah with his three-year-old daughter, Kelsey. He pointed to the candles and asked Kelsey, "What is that?"

"A menorah," she answered, as if surprised that her father didn't know it.

Peter then recited the proper blessing — in

Hebrew! From memory! When I expressed surprise, he told me the story of how the Maccabees reclaimed the Temple and found one jug of oil that somehow managed to last eight days. Where did he learn that?

My son Joel joined me for a couple of classes with Rabbi Aaron. Another surprise — I learned that he was attending some religious Shabbat meals around town. And now he is talking about going to study in Israel.

My son Eric had the greatest affinity for Judaism as a young boy. He even took bar mitzvah classes with a Reform rabbi, but never finished. He did a movie in Israel and picked up quite a bit of Hebrew. For my birthday a couple of years ago, he gave me a beautiful *tallis* he had flown over from Jerusalem. And, being a stand-up comedian some of the time, he invited me to a Yom Kippur service at the Comedy Club on Sunset Boulevard. Most recently, while in a drug rehabilitation center, he finally had a bar mitzvah.

But it was Michael who delivered the biggest surprise. And I never even suspected what he was up to.

One day he walked into my house. Seeing him always gave me a lift. We kissed each other on the mouth — Russian style.

I grabbed his biceps, which involuntarily flexed into a firm muscle. "Working out, Michael?"

"A little bit," he said.

I poked his pectorals, which bulged into hard mounds. "It's good to have strong peasant blood, huh, Mickey?"

"Yeah." He smiled and his white teeth glistened. "Good teeth, too."

"Dad, stop inspecting me like a horse."

"It's in the genes." I laughed as I clamped my teeth together with a loud click. "Your Russian grandfather never brushed his teeth in his life. He said, 'Brush teeth, teeth fall out.' And he never lost a tooth until he was seventy. He could take a cap off of a bottle with his teeth." (Michael had heard that story before, but that never stopped me from repeating it.) "I wouldn't try it if I were you because remember, on your mother's side — English — they were never known for good teeth."

The phone rang. It was for Michael. They must know where he is every minute of the day.

Michael makes a surprise visit on the set.
(*M. Pelletier/Sygma*)

I studied my oldest son animatedly talking on the phone. And I thought, My mother was right. America is such a wonderful land. You have a chance. My parents made that long voyage from White Russia and landed at Ellis Island. They were illiterate, but I had a chance to get a college education and go into the field of work that I wanted to pursue — acting. Now, standing at the telephone, making a multimillion dollar deal for another major motion picture, is my son, more famous than his father.

I had always wanted to make a movie with Michael. We talked about it often and looked at a lot of scripts that never seemed right. But, to be honest, we just weren't ready. Our relationship was evolving, and it would have been tough for us to handle the creative tension that comes with a major motion picture.

For a long time, Michael and I were not close. I always thought it went back to my divorce from his mother. He was a strange kid. When he was young, he never asked for anything. If I gave him money, he took it reluctantly, but never asked. This infuriated me. I used to say, "Michael, that's insulting. I'm your father, you should ask me for things."

Even when he was trying to get started in the movie business, he never asked for my help. He struggled on his own, and sometimes it was very hard to succeed in the shadow of a famous father. But eventually he overcame all the obstacles. He paid his dues and became extremely well respected on his own merit, not just because he was the son of

Kirk Douglas. Hell, he won two Oscars and is now getting $20 million a picture!

As I no longer felt I needed to play the role of the father — give him good advice (which he did not want) or run interference (which he absolutely hated) — I started to relax around him. And he, learning a thing or two about being a father himself, stopped being so hard on me.

I remember when his son Cameron got angry with him for being off somewhere making a movie. Michael told me the story and apologized for having done that a few times to me. Now he knew how it felt.

We became gentle with each other. Our new relationship was precious to us, and we didn't want to spoil it with a movie.

On my seventy-seventh birthday he gave me a very special gift.

He knew that I hate birthdays — they only depress me. I don't understand why everyone celebrates them. What's so special about a birthday? Every person, every animal and every building has one. Right now I couldn't tell you the birthdays of my six sisters. Most of the time I forget my own. Once, when I was in college, I didn't realize that my nineteenth birthday had passed until a week later.

I have to admit that I remembered very clearly when I reached my seventy-seventh birthday. I was in my office, a little sad about the passage of time. A Shakespearean sonnet floated through my mind: "I all alone beweep my outcast state, / And trouble deaf heaven with my bootless cries . . ." My secretary walked in and insisted that I follow her to the parking lot. I was perplexed and wondered why she was so excited.

In the middle of the parking lot was a shiny, new automobile. An Infiniti. With a red ribbon tied around it. Someone had been very thoughtful — this model had a special seat, particularly good for my bad back. I opened the door and sat down. On the steering wheel was a note. I recognized the handwriting. The note said:

Dear Dad,
    You say I never asked you for anything, but you gave me a lot. Happy birthday. I love you, Michael.

The car was nice, but that note — it made for a very special birthday present.

On my seventy-eighth birthday, he topped that. "Happy birthday, Dad," he said simply, and handed me a script. "It's a first draft of a movie, I hope we'll make it in nineteen ninety-five."

That night in bed I started reading it. It was called *A Song for David* and was written by Dan Gordon from his own life experiences. It was, of course, a father-son story. We always knew it would be. But it was extraordinary how close to home it hit. I was astounded.

First of all it was a Jewish story. My character, David, has rediscovered Judaism in his old age. Now it brings special meaning to his life and fills him with renewed energy. His son and partner,

Daniel, doesn't understand what's come over his father. Daniel is a workaholic who burns the midnight oil and drives a sedan, while his father pores over the Talmud with rabbis and drives a sports car. The clash between father and son happens over a playground that the father wants to build in the middle of a poor neighborhood on a site his son had earmarked for a shopping center. As father and son wrestle with each other, the father gets a brain tumor.

I won't go on, but I have to tell you that the story culminates with father and son in Israel, at the Israeli version of the Olympics, the Maccabiah Games.

I couldn't believe it. My boy, my son, gave me such a present. He had missed nothing of the hints I dropped about the Torah, my project of building parks for children. I was dumbfounded.

But the best part — and we both knew it — was that this was a great script. This was the movie for us!

I would be working with my son at last.

God had been good to me.

CHAPTER

NINETEEN

Michael is the only one of my four sons with whom I have never worked. How did he escape? I have acted with Eric several times, and appeared in movies produced by or with Joel and Peter.

I have never wanted any of my sons to be in my profession. It's so lonely, and the chances for success are so remote. I discouraged them from entering this world of make-believe and encouraged them to find other pursuits. Well, you see the strength of my influence.

When I realized there was no dissuading them, I began to fantasize about all of us working together. I could see it clearly. They'd all become part of the Bryna Company, named after their grandmother, and we'd start a dynasty of filmmakers.

But that was not to be either, although all of them worked with my company for short periods of time. They all got the hell out just as soon as they could. Now I understand why. Of course, every son has to find his own individuality. But back then I was hurt.

When Bryna made *Posse* in 1975, I took on too much — I starred in it, produced it and directed it. As a result, it was not the most soothing environment for my son Joel, who was my associate producer. One day I was out shooting on location near Tucson, Arizona, while Joel was in town working in the office. At the end of the day's shooting I came back to find Joel had skipped town. He had received a call from my son Michael, who offered him a job. It took Joel exactly twenty-nine minutes to pack and get the hell out. I was disappointed. Joel has a great sense of humor and was a lot of fun to be with, but I guess he didn't see me the same way.

Joel once confided in me that he used his sense of humor as a weapon to protect him from getting hurt. He is always cheery and ready with an amusing quip. He is like a big teddy bear, adorable and huggable.

When Michael was slated to make *Cutthroat Island*, a pirate movie with Geena Davis, Joel was named associate producer. But then I heard from Michael that the script wasn't good enough. I asked Joel what was the matter with it. "Well, Dad," he said, "Geena Davis gets to make like Errol Flynn and Michael gets to stand around and eat a banana." (Geena made the movie with Matthew Modine.)

I always have been surprised and delighted that Michael and Joel got along so well. It can be cold if you live too long in the shadow of a famous father and brother.

For a long time, Joel lived in France with his third wife, Patty, running a studio in Nice. This year we were all glad to have Joel come home. He had to have a hip replacement, which is a complicated procedure with a long recovery. His wife stayed in France — the first signal that the marriage was on the rocks.

Anne helped him translate all the French legal

papers for his divorce. He was always calling her for advice. As a matter of fact, he solicited her advice much more often than he did mine.

Peter, my third son, is a lot of fun too, but in a different way. He knows how to entertain and is a terrific host. He loves the best wine, food and clothing, and he knows how to live in style.

Peter, thank God, is happily married. His beautiful wife, Lisa, has just received her master's degree in kinesiology; she is a fitness buff and lifts weights daily. At our Palm Springs home, we have an exercise room with a sign over the door: LISA'S GYM. As you enter, you are greeted by a seven-foot poster of Lisa, scantily clad, showing off her musculature. I was a champion wrestler in college, but I would hesitate to take her on.

Lisa and Peter have two children, Kelsey Anne and Tyler Daniel. (Daniel is all that's left of my original name, Danielovitch.)

Children are a happy and sad reminder of the passage of time. It did not seem so long ago that Michael's son, Cameron, who is now eighteen, was a chubby baby. Now I see him holding his little cousin — he is so grown up and she is a chubby baby. How long before she will be bouncing off on her first date? She is so beautiful, with golden curls inherited from her father, and an expressive face with the peaches-and-cream complexion of her mother. Of course, she is my wife Anne's first grandchild. The relationship between the two of them is amazing. Anne will never forget the day Kelsey whispered in her ear, "Oma, you are spe-

Peter's beautiful wife, Lisa, with my grandchildren, Tyler (10 months) and Kelsey (4 years).

cial." Oma is the name she calls Anne, and she is always anxious to visit Oma's house; I wonder when she will learn it is also Pappy's house, the name she calls me.

Sometimes, when I look at Kelsey Anne, I think of what my rabbi, David Aaron, said: "Kirk, I need nothing more than to look at the sweet, beautiful face of my baby to know there is a God."

Peter was a very different child — the only one

who refused to go to college — and yet he is extremely bright. When he was twenty-three years old, he came up with a concept for my movie *The Final Countdown*, and arranged with the Navy to have it shot aboard the nuclear-powered aircraft carrier the U.S.S. *Nimitz*. I couldn't imagine my young son making deals with officers decorated with gold braid. But he did, and he became the producer.

Of course, he was very young to have such a responsible job, so he pretended to be older. The first week of shooting, his mother planned to visit us to celebrate our twenty-fifth wedding anniversary. Peter was alarmed. "Twenty-fifth? Dad, you can't do that. I've told everyone I'm twenty-six." I answered, "Don't worry, Peter, I'll tell them you were born out of wedlock."

We worked well together on a series of movies, including *Amos* and *Inherit the Wind*, for which Peter won an Emmy.

Working with Eric, my youngest son, was something else. He is the most unpredictable, exasperating, enchanting, infuriating person, but never dull. His life is in constant turmoil. For years he has been unable to decide whether to live in New York or in Los Angeles, so he lives in both places at the same time. I told him, "Eric, there is an old German expression — *Man kann nicht mit ein Popo auf zwei Hochzeiten bleiben* — 'with one ass you can't sit at two weddings.' " I'll be damned if Eric hasn't proven this to be false.

When he was very young he played a small part in

a movie I made with Johnny Cash, *A Gunfight,* and we worked together again in a movie I made in Israel, *Remembrance of Love.* Once I tried to advise him how to play a scene. His response: "Dad, you're not the director. You're just an actor." He was very difficult, but then he was a teenager. Later, we worked together in the *Tales from the Crypt* series for HBO, in an episode directed by Bob Zemeckis *(Back to the Future, Forrest Gump)* and also starring Dan Aykroyd. Fortunately, it was a short shooting schedule. We never would have lasted out a long one. Eric's acting was excellent, but he was still difficult. Afterward, we didn't talk to each other for weeks. Maybe the movie's ending had something to do with it — in the final scene I have him shot by a firing squad.

Eric has been in the news a lot because of his drug problem, and he has gotten into various scrapes with the law because of it. Right now he is in rehab, and we pray that it will help.

There is no doubt it's a mad, mad, mad world we live in. I feel sorry for the children born in such a world of hatred, racism and violence. But also, my heart goes out to the youngsters in the movie industry. I think of my four sons living in the fishbowl of the movie world. Believe me, the children of stars don't have an easy life.

At the age of thirty-two, Gregory Peck's son ended his life with a bullet. At a similar age, the son of a very dear friend of mine, the producer Ray Stark, jumped out of a window. Paul Newman's died of a drug overdose. Producer George

Englund's son died from the same thing. Marlon Brando's son murdered his sister's lover. She had been in and out of mental institutions; then she committed suicide. Louis Jourdan's son committed suicide by drowning. Carol Burnett's daughter overdosed on drugs. Charles Boyer's son, Carroll O'Connor's son — both took their own lives. And so it goes, on and on.

Of course, the world we live in makes it difficult for all children. Now, as I study the Torah, I wonder if some of the problems my children have had might have been alleviated if I had exposed them more to religion. Maybe all children need some form of spiritual guidance to help them. I don't mean the rote, ritualistic religion I was taught as a child; that had no significant value to me. I mean

Working with Eric in *Tales of the Crypt*. At the end of the film, I had him executed by a firing squad.
(*Cliff Lipson/HBO*)

the kind of religion that helps you push aside your ego to let something spiritual come in.

Could the pain of all those kids have been alleviated if they'd had some spiritual guidance? Would that have enabled them to endure and conquer their suffering instead of ending it by death? Maybe some form of organized religion would have enabled them to develop a sense of values and priorities, given them a better yardstick of measuring the worth of fame and fortune as well as failure.

All my kids have gone through some form of therapy. It helped Michael and Joel, both of whom checked into Sierra Tucson for alcohol abuse. There they had to learn that they could not solve their problems alone, that they needed the help of a higher force — God.

The twelve steps of Alcoholics Anonymous are predicated on a belief in God. While AA does not espouse any particular religion, it forces the addict to acknowledge that there is a Higher Power. He must admit to himself that he cannot find a solution without the help of this Higher Power. It is interesting that this treatment was inadvertently triggered by Carl Jung, one of the world's greatest psychologists.

Once, Jung tried to cure a patient of alcoholism but nothing worked, and he finally gave up. He told his patient that he could not help him, but suggested that some form of religious conversion might do the trick. It did, and his patient passed the cure to another, and he to Bill W., the founder of AA.

What could I have done differently to help my

sons with the problems that they have had in life? Believe me, my list is very long. But I also feel that if they had been born in a different home, they still would have ended up with more or less the same challenges in life.

I take great solace studying the Torah and learning how the great patriarchs raised their kids. Boy, did they have problems!

Abraham was the epitome of kindness. Unlike me, he never lost his temper. But at some point he had to throw his oldest son, Ishmael, out of the house. The kid was nothing but trouble. Even God told Abraham to send Ishmael packing.

Then we get Isaac. He had twins, a good son, Jacob, and a bad son, Esau. Okay, so Isaac was blind and maybe he didn't see what the kids were up to, but clearly Esau's evil character had little to do with his parents, and probably Jacob's good character didn't either. The Bible says that the brothers were already fighting each other in the womb — they were opposites from conception!

Take King David — great monarch, lousy father. His oldest son, Amnon, was a rapist. His third son, Absalom, was very handsome but very spoiled. He organized a full-scale revolt against his father. Caught totally unaware, David was forced to flee. Then a battle took place. David issued strict orders that Absalom was not to be killed. But, in the battle, Absalom's long, beautiful hair became entangled in the branches of a tree, and, trapped, he was killed by David's general. David cried, "My son Absalom, my son, my son!"

Can you blame David for his sons' behavior? He was also father to Solomon, the greatest king of the Jewish people and famous for his wisdom.

But Solomon's son and heir, Rehoboam, was a fool. He was also greedy and arrogant. He refused to cut back the heavy taxes levied on the people during the building of the Temple. He said, "My father made your yoke heavy, but I will add to your yoke; my father flogged you with whips, I will flog you with scorpions."

So how wise was Solomon as a father? Either not too wise, or he had no say in how his kids would turn out.

I could go on and on. Trust me, though. Your kids arrive in the hospital with plenty of baggage. You can help them carry it or you can add to their burden. Ultimately, though, it's up to them what they do with their lives.

But in my studies of the Torah I noticed one very interesting thing: What you bequeathed to your oldest son was of extreme importance — it could literally change history.

Although I never conferred the "blessing of the firstborn" on Michael, I noticed him taking on this mantle.

He was the first one to show interest in his lineage, badgering me with questions about the *shtetls* of Russia where his grandparents had lived. Years ago I asked him, "How do you see yourself, Michael? Who are you?"

He thought awhile and responded, "A Jew."

"Why?"

"Because I feel I am."

I pointed out to him that he didn't have to say that. "By Jewish law, you are what your mother is. Those old Jews were smart. They knew they could be sure about the mother, but they could never be positive who was the father."

"Don't be worried, Dad. People say I look like you."

We laughed.

Over the years, Michael has taken on the task of bringing the family together for various celebrations and holidays, often no small feat with Joel living in France and Eric acting in New York, but he pulled it off a few times.

He knew what it meant to me to sit at the head of the table, pretending to be a Jewish patriarch, enjoying my sons and my extended family. Often my ex-wife Diana (Michael and Joel's mother) and her husband Bill would be there as well. We always stayed good friends, which Michael appreciated very much.

Michael and I get together often. Sometimes we watch a ball game, sometimes we just talk. On one of those occasions I decided to give him a present.

"This is something I want you to have."

And I handed it to him. It was a primitive statue I had acquired some fifty years ago, a Cameroonian carving, about two feet tall, of a nude figure — one side had the female organs, the other the male.

He just looked at it quizzically. "You into idols now, Dad?"

"It's not an idol. It's a representation of the human psyche. I've kept this piece hidden because it makes some people uncomfortable."

"I can see why."

"But isn't it remarkable what these African natives knew so long ago — that every human being has a feminine as well as a masculine side."

Michael turned the figure over. "That's some statement from a macho guy like you, Dad."

"What macho?" I scoffed. "You kids grew up seeing me on the screen, shooting it out in a saloon, riding off into the sunset with the cowboys. But that was never the real me."

"Yeah, sure, Dad."

"You know, Michael, it's silly, but we see the cowboy as a symbol of macho, but he is not. Robert Johnson, the psychologist, said that half of the word cowboy is cow and the other half is boy — if he was really macho he'd be bullman."

"You got a point there."

"We're screwed up. But the primitive people who made this statue understood the complex nature of the human psyche much better. It's all about the balance between the feminine and the masculine. The feminine side is a symbol of creativity — it's what made you the fine actor that you are today. The masculine side gives you the perseverance, the strength to go on. Your sexuality."

Michael seemed very interested, or he was very good at pretending.

Touching the figure, I said, "You know why we are like that?"

"I have a feeling you're gonna tell me."

"It says in the Torah that Adam was both male and female —"

"You're kidding."

"— but God saw that this human creature was lonely without a companion."

"I didn't know that."

"Yeah, read it for yourself, it's in the book of Genesis, that's what it says . . . out of Adam God created Eve to become helpmate for him."

"That's very interesting."

I looked to see if he meant it. He did.

"In the Torah all the finer qualities of mankind are feminine. The *Shechinah* — the Holy Spirit of God — is feminine. *Binah,* understanding, is feminine, so is *chochmah,* wisdom, *gevurah,* strength, even the Hebrew word *Torah* is a feminine noun.

"It is the link to the feminine within himself that gives a man power — not brute force, but real strength that is the true opposite of weakness."

Michael listened to me thoughtfully. "That makes a lot of sense."

I thought later that if I were an old Jewish patriarch I would give Michael and all my sons a blessing that they should reconcile these feminine and masculine forces inside themselves, because in their balance lies true strength.

I also thought of what other blessings I would like to confer on my children. For my youngest and most troubled son, Eric, I would bless him to learn how to take blame and credit with equanimity and to control his impulsive nature. My son Peter I would bless to appreciate that all the beautiful things of life he enjoys are on loan to him from God; he should use them to make the world a better place. My son Joel I would bless that he should not despair when things don't go his way and learn to offset his loving, happy-go-lucky nature with a drive to make a difference in life. My son Michael I would bless with more joy and less guilt; he has paid his dues and earned the right to enjoy his accomplishments.

My children have blessed me too.

Once when Peter was taking his daughter Kelsey camping, I told him that seeing what a good father he was made me feel guilty. "I never took you camping, Peter."

"Yeah," he said, "but you took me to Rome, London and to Paris. That wasn't too bad."

When I was feeling depressed after a series of health setbacks, Joel wrote me a beautiful letter. He said:

Dear Dad,

I've been thinking about you a lot in the past few weeks. I've been thinking of all the things you've accomplished, and I think of the things you are still accomplishing, but you for some reason don't believe it . . .

There is a major difference between depression and frustration. Depression is to give up and acknowledge failure. But frustration is a driving force in life. Be frustrated, not depressed. Not you, not with what you have done, and are now doing.

I love you and I'm proud of the old man.

And I was overwhelmed when Michael said to me, "Dad, you have been a wonderful father."

I was startled. "Me? The wild man?"

"Yeah, you. I didn't think I would need a father when I was fifty. But you were there when I needed you."

"Wow, Michael. Would you write that in a letter 'to whom it may concern'?"

"No, *that* I will write in a letter to you."

It took me fifty years to become a father, but I did it.

CHAPTER

TWENTY

And yet, something tells me that one award I'll never get is Father of the Year. At least I can take consolation in the fact that I've been given a lot of others. Now, before you get the wrong impression, I'm not bragging. Charitable organizations have discovered that giving an award to a celebrity at a dinner in his or her honor makes for a successful fund-raiser.

In fact, so many organizations have now established annual awards that they are quite aggressively competing for celebrities to honor. Several times I've received letters offering to recognize my contributions in fighting a disease I have never even heard of.

Another type of award that is given all too frequently is the lifetime-achievement award. Whenever I get one of those I feel uncomfortable. I always imagine the committee looking at my medical records, saying, "My God, we've got to give this guy an award quick! Look at this! Helicopter accident, pacemaker, bad back, bad knees. We better move fast!"

Why do they have to call these things "*lifetime-* achievement awards"? Can't they call it just a plain "achievement award"? What makes them decide that a person's lifetime is over, that his achievements are finished?

I always feel like shouting, "My lifetime isn't up yet! I have many things I still want to achieve! I'm not nearly done!"

Besides making you feel like you're finished, awards can get you in a lot of trouble. Let me tell you . . .

We've had a house in Palm Springs for over thirty years, and we love it. During the winter season we take advantage of the beautiful desert weather just about every weekend, and, of course, we try to be good citizens of that little town in the Coachella Valley. We've helped the hospital and the museum; we put in new sewers; we organized a project to take down telegraph poles; and we assisted in many other civic causes, just as good citizens should.

But as the saying goes, "No good deed goes unpunished."

For years, I declined the invitation to be honored as Palm Springs's Citizen of the Year. The idea embarrassed me. But they kept insisting — the luncheon at which I would be honored was another way of raising money for the chamber of commerce — and, finally, I agreed.

The event was a big success; the auditorium was packed. During the festivities, it was announced that in my honor one of the main streets, El Cielo Drive, would now become Kirk Douglas Boulevard. I liked that idea — it appealed to my ego.

But the chamber of commerce had neglected to tell the residents of El Cielo about the change. They lived on a street named after the sky; now they'd be living on a street named after an actor. And sure enough, as soon as the story hit the papers, a swell of controversy arose that developed into a tidal wave of protest against the proposed change. The merchants said their customers wouldn't be able to find their stores. Others objected to having to absorb the cost of new stationery and business cards.

As letters to the editor of the local newspaper poured in against it, so did those for my defense. One famous Palm Springs resident, the former Dallas Cowboys quarterback Don Meredith, said, "Only a street named for Kirk Douglas? How about a mountain?"

I solved the problem by telling the chamber of commerce: "I changed my name before, I'll change it again. Just call me Kirk El Cielo."

So, if you should visit Palm Springs, be sure to drive down the street named after me.

After the Palm Springs fiasco, I swore I would not accept any more awards. But then . . .

The announcement from the John F. Kennedy Center for the Performing Arts came on very fancy stationery. Yes, they wished to honor me for "lifetime contributions to dramatic arts."

The Kennedy Center Honors are awards given by the nation with accolades at the White House and at the State Department before the final gala at the Kennedy Center itself. Something like that you don't say no to. Something like that you have to go and accept.

Still, I had my usual misgivings. The dreaded picture leapt into my mind — an august committee hemming and hawing over my medical records, finally deciding they couldn't put it off for another year — a grim prophecy of doom . . .

I shouldn't joke about this. At the time of this writing, there is an uncomfortable correlation between awards and disasters in my life.

Shortly after the announcement that I was to receive the American Film Institute award for lifetime achievement, I was in the helicopter crash. Shortly after the announcement that I was to receive an Oscar for lifetime achievement, I had a stroke. Fortunately, the Kennedy Center announcement was not followed by a calamity.

But I had no idea that this boost to my ego would, in a strange way, affect my spiritual life.

I told my wife that this was a terrific award because I didn't have to worry about making an acceptance speech. You just sit there looking modest and humble. Anne replied, "That's a role you can't play." Was she joking?

There is a lot of buzz about the Kennedy Center Honors. The tickets for the Sunday-night performance are gobbled up immediately by East Coast society at a minimum of $1,500 per ticket, $5,000 for a box seat. The rest of the country and the people who can't afford a ticket can see the performance for nothing when it's on television three weeks later.

My sons were proud and would certainly all be there in Washington for the event. For me, getting my sons all together in one room is quite an award in itself. Of course, it didn't turn out that way. My son Joel could not get to Washington — he had to stay in Los Angeles, hobbling in a walker, recovering from his hip-replacement operation. But Michael, Peter and Eric were there, as well as my daughters-in-law Diandra and Lisa and my grandson Cameron.

The festivities started Saturday night. My family and I left the Ritz-Carlton Hotel and headed for the State Department, a beautiful building filled with glorious American antiques, each piece of furniture a collector's item. I was breathless standing before the desk where Thomas Jefferson wrote the Declaration of Independence. He had designed the desk himself so that he could sit and write or, with a small adjustment, could stand and write. Maybe he had a bad back too.

There was an amazing mixture of stars and political figures in attendance. My old buddy Lauren Bacall ("Betty" to her friends) sat next to me. Of course, I had no idea that she would be participating in the gala performance the next night. Details of the show were very hush-hush. I had asked Michael why they hadn't asked him to do something. He just shrugged and said, "I don't know." Of course, he was the star attraction in the segment about me.

At the dinner table, Peter, contrary to protocol,

pulled out his portable phone and called Joel, who had been left behind. All of us took turns speaking to him.

After dinner, the awards were presented. The other recipients that year were: Morton Gould, the composer; Harold Prince, the Broadway producer; Aretha Franklin, soul singer; and Pete Seeger, rebel folksinger. The chairman of the Kennedy Center, James D. Wolfensohn, came to the table of each honoree to hang a medal around his or her neck. It was strange-looking — the multicolored wide ribbon had frayed edges and gold bars at the lapel level that looked like clothespins.

Then someone stepped up to the podium to propose a brief toast to each honoree. My friend Jack Valenti raised his glass to me.

Earlier, he had told me that he wanted to relate the story of my breaking the Hollywood blacklist. "It's such an old story," I said. But he insisted that it was part of Americana and deserved to be repeated. So he told the group about how I decided to put Dalton Trumbo's name on the *Spartacus* script because I was so angry that everyone was using him as a writer but changing his name because he was blacklisted. (Trumbo even won an Oscar under an assumed name; of course, he couldn't go and pick it up.) I caught a lot of flak for what I did at the time, but the blacklist was broken. When Jack finished telling the story I was surprised to find that people acted like this was a startling piece of news. It happened more than thirty years ago!

When all the awards had been handed out, the

How dignified we are — recipients of Kennedy Center Honors — me, Aretha Franklin, Pete Seeger and (in front) Harold Prince, Morton Gould. (© *Joan Marcus*)

honorees were corralled into the foyer and roped off from the other guests, who stood gawking at us, while a battery of photographers took pictures. With the heavy medallions dangling around our necks like yokes on oxen, we must have looked pretty ridiculous, but we all tried to appear serious and deserving.

But the oddest thing was not the award, but the box it came in. It weighed a ton. And I have to tell you the medallion looked much better lying inside, as you peered at it through the glass top, than it did around my neck.

(But then most awards are silly-looking. Look at the Oscar. A heavy sculpture of a man with his arms crossed, holding a sword. Why a man? Why a sword? Years ago, I received the Oscar equivalent in Paris; over there, it's called a César. It looks like a bunch of crushed tin cans.)

The next day, at the White House, I stood with my fellow honorees in front of a large Christmas tree in the Blue Room, which by the way is now painted pink. I have been to the White House more than a few times, but it is always an exciting experience. I found myself rubbing the moisture from my palms on my pants as I stood waiting for the President and Mrs. Clinton to greet us. I tried to think of something clever to say. As the head of our country shook my hand, I said, "Standing before this Christmas tree gives me the opportunity to wish you a Happy Hanukkah." The President gave me a blank stare — he must have been thinking of Bosnia. I felt foolish, but didn't explain that it was the seventh night of Hanukkah.

We marched into the Green Room (which is still green) and sat on a dais in front of a select group of friends and officials. The President spoke. I don't remember what he said, but I didn't forget that he said his administration would end either like *Gunfight at the O.K. Corral* or *Spartacus*.

I was very flattered.

Before leaving for the Kennedy Center gala, everyone headed for the buffet table. I left my wife to pay my respects to Mr. and Mrs. Wolfensohn, who were standing in the crowded foyer chatting with another couple. As I spoke to the Wolfensohns, I noticed their eyes darting away. I turned and found that I had ignored Vice-President Al Gore and his wife, Tipper. Again, I felt foolish and tried to apologize. I removed myself awkwardly and went back to my wife. When I told her about my embarrassment, she sighed and said, "I can't take you anywhere."

I was pleasantly surprised to be sitting next to Hillary Clinton in the Presidential Box. Boy, if the guys in Amsterdam could see me now, looking down at the commoners in their $1,500 orchestra seats.

On the other side of me sat Pete Seeger, who had been blacklisted for seventeen years during the McCarthy era. What wonderful songs he wrote: "If I Had a Hammer," "Where Have All the Flowers Gone" — songs that have always had a deep meaning for me.

I was beginning to feel very comfortable as I leaned back and enjoyed the first segment — a tribute to Aretha Franklin. But I wasn't prepared for what came next. First, I saw Lauren Bacall strut across the stage to the podium. She said nothing to me at dinner about having a part in the show. Here's a girl who can keep a secret. Leaning on the podium, she conjured up warm memories about our days at the American Academy of Dramatic Arts in New York, when I tried to seduce her on a rooftop in Greenwich Village (without success). Then she narrated a film montage. The clips from my movies didn't impress me; I'd seen them before. But they had some photos that were very touching — one of my mother and me, another of a scene from a college production of *Death Takes a Holiday* in which I looked like my grandson.

And then three actors — Alan Alda, Ron Silver and Tom Skerritt — took turns reading segments of my autobiography, *The Ragman's Son*. Alan ended by reading the last part of my book:

I am walking briskly to my Beverly Hills office on a beautiful day, feeling alive after my early-morning workout with Mike Abrums, who has just told me that I look better now than I did in *Champion*, forty years ago. The California sun is warm on my skin, the purple trumpets of the jacarandas are music to my eyes. I am eager to hear the response of yet another studio executive to a script I own, a picture I have tried to make for years, a role I want to play very much.

I dash across Wilshire Boulevard, wave back to some hardhat construction workers. I answer the call of a passing taxi driver — "Hi, Spartacus!" I think I hear a timid voice say "Mr. Douglas," but keep on walking. The timid voice becomes a little stronger — "Mr. Douglas." I stop and turn and see a very pretty, tall, young blond girl wearing shorts.

I can spare a minute of my time for her, a fan hoping for my autograph; perhaps an aspiring actress who wants the benefit of my expertise. After all, I have lasted more than forty years in Hollywood, where stars come and go. Not bad for the ragman's son. All my life, I always knew I would be somebody. Wasn't I born in a gold box? And now, the rest of the world knows who I am too.

She looks up at me adoringly with eyes the color of jacaranda blossoms.

I suck in my gut, puff out my chest, slap a biceps.

In a velvet voice, she says, "Wow! Michael Douglas's father!"

On that note, Michael walked onto the stage. (My son! He's got two of those guys leaning on a sword!)

Michael began by saying warm things about me. And a funny feeling started to creep over me. Take it easy, Kirk, I said to myself. Spartacus doesn't cry. And I held it back. Michael talked about a lullaby that my mother sang to me in Yiddish, *"Rozhinkes mit Mandlen"* ("Raisins and Almonds"), a song that brings sweet dreams. I had visions of blubbering all over the First Lady's velvet gown. I was determined not to give in. But then I heard a flute playing the tune, and about fifty children walked out onstage singing. Listening to the song that I had heard so often many, many years ago, I suddenly knew the meaning of "voices of angels." Those sweet sounds seemed to fill every part of me. I closed my eyes to hold back the tears and saw visions of my mother blessing the Friday-evening Shabbat candles.

On Saturday morning, she would be so neatly dressed, her hair combed perfectly, as she'd sit in a rocking chair on the front porch with her arms folded. She looked so peaceful. It was an unusual sight. There was a holiness about my mother. And as that song about raisins and almonds floated up to me, I thought, My God, how far away I've strayed. Right then and there, I made a promise to start lighting candles every Friday night.

Later, my wife told me that the First Lady was

My grandson Cameron, Michael's son, came to see the old man get a pat on the back.

223

carefully watching me as I tried unsuccessfully to hold back my tears. As I stood up to take a bow, I knew that TV cameras were aimed at me from somewhere. I was determined — they mustn't see me wiping my eyes. I felt my wife's reassuring clasp on my arm as I looked down into the faces of the audience and spotted Peter and Eric looking up at me.

That night, as I lay in bed, the wonderful events of the evening kept tumbling in my mind. There were so many memorable moments, but crowning them all was my grandson Cameron throwing his arms around me and whispering in my ear: "Pappy, I'm so proud that you're my grandfather."

CHAPTER

TWENTY-ONE

Following the Kennedy Center Honors I resolved to start lighting Shabbat candles every Friday night. I remembered my mother's candlesticks, which she had brought over from Russia; I was sure they had been packed away somewhere. My sisters were not religious, but they wouldn't have given something like that away.

I called my sister Fritzie.

She remembered that the candlesticks had gone to the oldest, Betty, who died some years ago. Perhaps her son Robert had them. I hoped that he had not disposed of them, and, with some trepidation, I called him.

"Hi, Robert. Do you remember your grandmother's candlesticks?"

"Sure do."

"Well, if you can find them, I would be grateful. I want to have them."

There was an awkward pause. "Uncle Kirk, I'm looking at them right now. I light them every Friday."

I was extremely touched. They had gone to the right person, who never put them away in some dusty corner, but used them every Shabbat just the way my mother did.

When I told Ushi about the story, she gave me a beautiful set of silver candlesticks she had bought in Jerusalem, and I began this special ritual.

Every Friday evening at sunset I light my candles and say the prayer that my mother used to say so many years ago. It gives me a wonderful, warm feeling to watch the burning candles, and, as my eyes narrow, it seems that the flames form two golden strands of light that reach up to heaven. At that moment, I am very close to my mother.

At that moment I am also very grateful to God for having brought me to this place and for having given me so many *naches* in my life. I tell Him I will pay Him back — when Michael and I make *Song for David*, it should give Judaism a big boost.

I wish I had discovered the beauty of my religion earlier in life. I feel sad for the time I have lost, and when I think about that, I feel extremely resentful of the Jewish teachers of my childhood, who put such an emphasis on the form and fundamentalism of the religion, but not on the spirituality. In my day, all the emphasis was on reading Hebrew but never on understanding it. So a young Jewish boy could be filled with all kinds of rules that he never understood, prayers that he never knew the meaning of, and it might take him years — as it took me — to begin to read translations of some of these prayers and realize the truth and beauty of what is in them.

The Jews have a prayer for everything. There are prayers recited before eating bread or vegetables or fruit. There is a prayer before drinking wine or even water. There is a prayer to be recited when

I never miss lighting candles for Shabbat.

smelling pleasing scents, when seeing the ocean, the mountains or a rainbow. The Jews sanctify everything in life. Even the most mundane is not forgotten. What other religion has a prayer for going to the toilet? You wince when you read the work "toilet," because you go to the rest room or men's room, or ladies' room or powder room, but you *never* go to the toilet. Our culture prefers the euphemisms because we are too embarrassed to refer too plainly to our bodily function. But going to the toilet is an act, which, if not performed regularly, can spell real trouble. Those old Jews knew that a long time ago. They said that a body without a soul is a corpse, but a soul without a body is just a ghost. They had high respect for the human body. The Talmud says, "Don't be embarrassed about your body — in striving for the holiness of the soul, don't forget the holiness of the body."

What's great about Judaism is that it always has its

feet on the ground, even while aspiring to the loftiest of heights. It is wise yet dramatic, poignant yet never without a sense of humor, and always full of surprises. I was astounded to learn that there is a commandment to get drunk during the festival of Purim. (Yes, you read it right — a commandment.) A Jew must imbibe so much liquor during Purim that he can't tell the difference between "Cursed be Haman" (who, like Hitler, wanted to destroy all the Jews) and "Blessed be Mordecai" (who, along with Queen Esther, foiled Haman's plot). This is to drive home the point that evil and good work go hand in hand in God's unfathomable plan; often, we choose good only when confronted with evil. An incredible insight!

People often assume — because of my age — that fear of death brought me back to Judaism, but they are mistaken. I am not someone trying to buy passes into heaven. (In fact, I am not always sure there is such a place.)

But, through the study of Torah, I have come to realize that when God created the first human being, He breathed something of Himself into each one of us. We have a tiny particle, a sliver, a little spark of God inside of us. And we must nurture that little spark into a flame that brings the light of God into the world.

I realized we don't do enough of that in our lives. Most of us don't set aside time — like a good Jew does every Sabbath — to reflect on the spiritual side of life.

There is no day more special than the seventh — maybe Yom Kippur, which is called the "Shabbat of Shabbats" — when we welcome the bride of Sabbath with song as we face toward Jerusalem. *Every week*, we experience the holiest of holy days.

If each one of us, especially those in leadership positions throughout the globe, really observed the Sabbath — whether, like the Moslems, they chose to do it on Friday, or, like the Jews, on Saturday or, like the Christians, on Sunday — and made it a day of rest and reflection, I'm sure it would make for a better world.

What a phony I am. Here I have given you a sermon on the importance of keeping the Sabbath, yet for years and years I never saw the inside of the synagogue on that holy day. I'm still not that good a Jew; you won't find me in shul all that often. But HaShem is a forgiving God and often rewards me when I do go. Not long ago, I took my wife to a Friday evening service conducted by Rabbi Joseph Telushkin, a great guy and a great writer, at the Synagogue for the Performing Arts. As I sat there in the front row, not so attentively listening to his sermon, I glanced over my shoulder and I saw the most beautiful girl in the world. It startled me. I turned back to listen to the sermon, but I didn't hear a word he was saying. Furtively, I took another look; she was still beautiful, and looked vaguely familiar.

I nudged my wife and whispered in her ear, "Do you see that beautiful girl behind you?"

She nodded.

"Who is she?"

She shrugged.

The rabbi finished his sermon, and came over to greet me and my wife. And then he greeted the beautiful girl and her male companion like old friends. I was startled and now even more curious. Finally I got the rabbi to the side. "Rabbi, who is that girl?"

His eyes widened. "Don't you know her? That's Michelle Pfeiffer."

Boy, it certainly increased my desire to go to the synagogue more often.

(It turned out that Michelle Pfeiffer was there that night because her husband, producer David E. Kelley, was developing a screenplay with the rabbi. Maybe Michelle will convert to Judaism — what a boost that would be for the Jews.)

Another time, on Yom Kippur, I was again sitting in the front row, waiting for the service to start when an attractive girl walked past me and sat down. I didn't want to be accused of ogling every sexy girl I see, although I must admit I do. (Of course, in an Orthodox synagogue men and women are seated separately to prevent just this kind of thing.) I controlled myself until the music of Kol Nidre started and she began sobbing. Now I looked at her more closely — it was Bette Midler.

Outside the synagogue, Judaism has nothing against looking at a beautiful woman, but don't touch. That is a law — often disobeyed — called *shomer n'gia,* which loosely translated means "Don't touch the merchandise," or as those crude people like me would say, "No hoopie, no shtuppie."

By the way, why is it that I meet the most beautiful girls when my wife is around? I often wonder. Last week, we were on the way to Montecito to see our grandchildren in my wife's flashy BMW sports car — I gave it to her for a birthday present.

We were surprised to see that we were running out of gas. Our housekeeper, Fifi, usually keeps the tank full, but she was on vacation. (You see how the rich live!) We pulled up to a gas station that had no full service, just self-service. We got out of the car, and I'm embarrassed to say we couldn't figure out how to open the gas tank. We must have appeared lost because a friendly driver came up to us and solved our problem. You just pull open the cover and the gas tank is exposed. I think that's just too simple for such a fancy car.

Apparently having no confidence in us, he also took the pump and filled up the tank, talking gaily as he did so. He was a professional chauffeur and pointed to the limo he was driving, next to which stood his client, a young woman. I walked closer — she was a vision and I was not in shul.

"What do you do?" I am always so subtle when I begin a conversation.

"I'm an actress," she replied modestly.

"Hmm," I growled, trying to act like a man who was impervious to her beauty. "You should be a schoolteacher." And I returned to our car now filled with gas.

A few weeks later, Anne came to me with a newspaper and several magazines featuring that year's hit of the Cannes Film Festival. "Isn't that the girl at the gas station?" she said.

I looked at the picture. It sure was. Her name was Liv Tyler — what a beauty!

But we Jews have always been intrigued with beautiful women. In the Bible we read about Bathsheba, Sarah, Queen Esther — all great beauties, but my favorite is Rachel.

When Jacob first met her at the well, he couldn't resist — he kissed her. That violates the law of *shomer n'gia*, but he couldn't help himself.

By the way, it's interesting that three of the Bible greats — Isaac, Jacob and Moses — found their wives at the well. Even Jesus met a woman — a prostitute — at the well. Maybe that's why they say, "Don't go to the well too often."

It sure got Jacob in trouble. He asked for Rachel's hand in marriage and her father insisted that he work seven years for her. He did. And you know what happened? At the marriage ceremony the bride came in with her face covered as was the custom, but, unbeknown to Jacob, it wasn't Rachel under the veil, but her older sister, Leah. Poor Jacob discovered the sabotage on the morning after he had consummated the marriage. Now he had to work seven more years for his true love, Rachel, though he was permitted to marry her a week later. And then Jacob lived with his two wives and two concubines for many years and had twelve sons and one daughter. Those were the days!

We Jews are ready to pay a big price for beauty,

but we place a higher value on intelligence. In the poverty-stricken community in which I was brought up, the highest accolade would be paid to the *chochem* — the wise man. On the bottom of the totem pole was the *narr* — the fool. A dumb Jew was an oxymoron.

I must confess I knew one dumb Jew; he worked for me. One day his assignment was to place my two young sons, Peter and Eric, on a plane at LAX, and I would pick them up in New York, where I was making *The Brotherhood.* This foolish Jew got carried away by the amenities of the VIP lounge, so while eating and drinking, he failed to put my children on the plane. Unaware of this, I was anxiously pacing at JFK in New York.

When the filming was over and I got back to Los Angeles, I had a talk with him. He tried to apologize but I cut him off. "You are dumb. A Jew has no right to be dumb. Where would we be now? We would never have survived if we were dumb. You're fired."

But don't get me wrong. I don't mean to exaggerate. There *are* dumb Jews — we find a famous one in the Bible. Samson. Oh yes, he has muscles in every part of his body, including his head.

The strongest Jew we ever had, and he goes and falls for the Philistine beauty Delilah. Every man has his weakness, of course, and she knows it. She pleads with him to know the source of his strength. But he lies to her. "Tie me with new rope," he tells her, "and I will be as weak as an ordinary man." She ties him up while he is asleep and has a Philistine ambush waiting. But Samson snaps the ropes. Again she asks

233

him to reveal the source of his strength, and again he lies. Again the ambush fails. Three times this happens.

Now Delilah pulls out that age-old trick. She says, "If you really love me, you'd trust me."

You'd think that after three betrayals, he'd have learned his lesson. No-o-o-o. He tells her that the secret of his strength is his long hair.

So — surprise, surprise — while Samson is sleeping, she gets a pair of scissors.

Poor Samson. The only dumb Jew in the entire Bible. But there is a postscript to the story. The Philistines were dumber. They threw him in the dungeon, but forgot to send in a barber to keep his hair cut. When his hair grew back . . . ah . . . go read the story for yourself.

Do you think I'm arrogant? Do you think I exaggerate the intelligence of the Jews? Perhaps. But please consider our history. The wandering Jew is kicked around from country to country for thousands of years. He clings tenaciously to his Judaism by studying the Torah day in and day out, often by candlelight, in some impoverished *shtetl*. He studies and debates the meaning of God's laws, sharpens his intellect — and eureka! — he gets smarter and so do his kids.

How many Jews do you think are in the entire world? Don't guess. I will tell you — about seventeen million. Yes, that's all. And of course you know that there are about two billion Christians, about one billion Moslems. So the Jews represent "a nebulous dim puff of star dust lost in the blaze of the Milky Way." I didn't say it. Mark Twain, not a Jew, said it. He wrote:

If the statistics are right, the Jews constitute but one quarter of one percent of the human race. It suggests a nebulous dim puff of star dust lost in the blaze of the Milky Way. Properly, the Jew ought hardly to be heard of; but he is heard of, has always been heard of. He is as prominent on the planet as any other people, and his importance is extravagantly out of proportion to the smallness of his bulk.

His contributions to the world's list of great names in literature, science, art, music, finance, medicine and abstruse learning are also very out of proportion to the weakness of his numbers. He has made a marvelous fight in this world in all ages; and has done it with his hands tied behind him. He could be vain of himself and be excused for it. The Egyptians, the Babylonians and the Persians rose, filled the planet with sound and splendour; then faded to dream-stuff and passed away; the Greeks and the Romans followed and made a vast noise, and they are gone; other peoples have sprung up and held their torch high for a time but it burned out, and they sit in twilight now, or have vanished.

The Jew saw them all, survived them all, and is now what he always was, exhibiting no decadence, no infirmities of age; no weakening of his parts, no slowing of his energies, no dulling of his alert and aggressive mind. All things are mortal but the Jew; all other forces pass, but he remains. What is the secret of his immortality?

And there is also this:

The Jew has brought down from heaven the everlasting fire and has illuminated with it the entire world.

I didn't say it, Leo Tolstoy, who wasn't a Jew, said it.

And then there is this:

Certainly the world without the Jews would have been a radically different place . . . To them we owe the idea of equality before the law, both divine and human, of the sanctity of life and the dignity of the human person, of the individual conscience and so of personal redemption; of the collective conscience and so of social responsibility; of peace as an abstract ideal and love as the foundation of justice and many other items which constitute the basic moral furniture of the human mind. Without the Jews, it might have been a much emptier place.

I didn't say that either. Paul Johnson, the famed historian, not a Jew, said it.

And lastly, how about this:

I will insist that the Hebrews have done more to civilize men than any other nation . . . fate had ordained the Jews to be the most essential instrument for civilizing the nations.

Not mine either. John Adams, the second president of the United States, not a Jew, said it.

So why have we been so hated? Why have we been constantly persecuted? Why have we been murdered, shot, hanged, burned, over and over and over again, throughout the ages? We are so few in number, why make of us even fewer? Why obliterate us? Would the world really be a better place without Jews?

CHAPTER

TWENTY-TWO

And yet . . .

Anti-Semitism has helped the Jews. In a strange way, anti-Semitism is responsible for the very survival of Judaism.

See, nothing can destroy the Jews, really. We have God's promise on that. God said to Abraham: *"I will establish My covenant between Me and you and your descendants after you throughout their generations — an eternal covenant . . ."*

The same promise is repeated over and over throughout the Bible, so it's a safe bet that the Jews will survive.

The catch is that sometimes we Jews forget we are Jews. When things are going well, we have a tendency to forget our special obligation to bring the light of God into the world — no easy task — and instead we try to slip quietly into the comfortable womb of assimilation.

Do you know which country has the best record of accepting Jews into every stratum of society?

Until 1492, that honor belonged to Spain. During the Golden Age of Spain, Jews prospered, much as they do in America today. Their prosperity led to assimilation and conversion to Christianity. Then the Inquisition hit. Initially it was aimed at ferreting out heretics, Jews who were not sincere converts, but by 1492, the tentacles of the Inquisition reached *all* Jews; they were robbed of their wealth and thrown out of a country they thought of as their own.

But the world moves on, people become enlightened, and within a few hundred years another country arose that claimed the best record of accepting Jews into every stratum of society.

Germany.

Of course, the Jews who made it in Germany could not be *obviously* Jewish. They had to walk, talk and dress like their Christian or secular colleagues. Reform Judaism got started in Germany as a way of being Jewish in a Christian environment. Hebrew prayers were translated into German, church organs were brought in, and the observance of the Sabbath was changed from Saturday to Sunday. But what might have started with good intentions quickly slid down a very slippery path. Soon, the reformers were describing themselves not as Jews but as "Germans of the Mosaic persuasion" and declaring, in the words of Reform Rabbi Abraham Geiger, that "Berlin is our Jerusalem." Before long they even devalued the Torah, saying it was some manuscript written by the ancients, certainly not the instructions for living from God, as Jews had maintained for three thousand years.

All the while these sophisticated German Jews kept distancing themselves from the *shtetl* Jews, who still followed the law of Moses, the *Halakhah*, like my ancestors who came from the Pale of

Settlement part of Russia.

Isn't it strange that Hitler should spring up in the country where so many Jews were removing themselves from Judaism?

I said before that nothing can destroy the Jews. But sometimes I think that nothing can destroy the Jews but the Jews.

In retrospect, it seems almost a black comedy. These misguided people, who were trying so hard to get away from Judaism, suddenly found themselves confronting a Nazi pointing a finger at them, saying: "You are a Jew."

They may have converted, they might have done everything to get rid of their Jewishness, but they were still stamped as Jews.

When Jews forget they are Jews, their enemies always remind them.

Hitler imposed on the German Jews all the things many were trying to give up through assimilation. He identified them with a Star of David and put them all together in a ghetto, a Jewish community. They had no way of forgetting who they were.

A few years ago, I happened to be in Paris on Yom Kippur, and my friend George Cravenne (whose family name once upon a time was Cohen) took me to his synagogue. I was surprised that he could not read the Hebrew text that I had been taught as a child. When I asked him about it, he confessed to me that he was never even bar mitzvahed. "I was not brought up Jewish in any way. For a long time, I didn't even think of myself as a Jew."

"But yet," I said, "I see you have your own prayer

shawl. You always go to the synagogue on Yom Kippur. You fast. When did you become Jewish?"

He smiled wanly. "When the Nazis almost captured me five different times in Paris. That made me a Jew."

What a peculiar reaction, and yet not uncommon.

I would hate to believe that we *need* anti-Semitism to exist, but it is strange that the most calculated attempt at destroying all the Jews — which nearly succeeded — only rekindled the faith of the Jewish people.

Those returning to Judaism — and Orthodox Judaism at that — have become a phenomenon. It's called the *ba'al t'shuva* movement. The movement of the returned ones.

Rabbi Joseph Telushkin, in his must-read work *Jewish Literacy*, explains how the Holocaust changed Jewish minds about their religion: "For decades, large numbers of Jews associated religiosity with intellectual backwardness, while associating secularism with modernity and sophistication. After World War II, it was apparent that nothing taught at Germany's great universities had inhibited German intellectuals from supporting the mass murder of the Jews."

In a perverse ratio, anti-Semitism brings out the best in Jews. If there was no anti-Semitism, Jews might disappear through assimilation, which by the way is doing quite a bit of damage to the Jewish population of America today. (I should know. I am one of the guilty ones, having been married twice, both times to non-Jewish women.)

Consider that two thousand years ago, at the time of the Roman Empire when records were meticulously kept, there were two million Jews. Today, by the most conservative estimates there should be two hundred million Jews, but there are only about seventeen million. That is what pogroms, the Inquisition, the Crusades and the

With my bride of 43 years.

Holocaust have done.

But in America there have been no mass persecutions that claimed lives. Fifty years ago, our census showed there were five million American Jews. Today, again by the most conservative estimates, there should be twelve million. But there are only six million. What pogroms haven't accomplished, assimilation has.

This morning, I picked up *The New York Times* and read the poignant story of our secretary of state, Madeleine Albright. She told interviewers that she had always assumed she was born a Catholic in Czechoslovakia, which she left with her family at age eleven in 1948; she remembered her parents recounting Christmas celebrations that they had experienced in their youth. But a careful study of her background, when she was confirmed for her cabinet post, revealed that both her parents were Jews and that her grandparents had been killed in the Holocaust. Her parents had fabricated an entire background. What a traumatic revelation!

But how many Jews throughout the years have done the same? How many have fabricated a life to protect themselves, and how many have failed? Are there many Christians today who know in their heart of hearts that they are Jews? Of course, there are many Jews who have freely converted to Christianity and vice versa. God has given us free will. But how tragic to have to live a lie or later on in life to find out that your parents created that lie. But do I condemn them? No. Haven't I once said that I was "half-Jewish" when I was in no danger of being put in an oven? I wrote about this dilemma in my first novel, wondering how many Jews still echo what my character, little Moishe, said — "Let's not be Jews."

There is a common Yiddish expression — *schwer zu sein a yid* — "it's tough to be a Jew." No wonder that some Jews don't want to be Jews. How would you like to go through your life carrying so much baggage?

I can understand my grandson's dilemma.

When Cameron was about eight, he came to Michael with a look on his face that showed he was grappling with a problem. "Pappy is Jewish, right, Dad?"

"That's right, Cameron."

"But what are you, Daddy?"

"I guess people would say that I'm half-Jewish."

"Oh." He tried to absorb that. "And what am I?"

"Well, you're a quarter-Jewish."

Cameron thought for a moment and then looked up at his father. "Daddy, I wanna be half-Jewish."

More recently, as a teenager, Cameron has learned that being Jewish in this world is not exactly a desirable characteristic. It occurred to him what occurred to me a few times in my lifetime — maybe it's better not to admit your lineage. He said to Michael, "You don't look Jewish and I don't look Jewish."

"I don't know what it means to look Jewish, but a part of you is."

"Yeah, but I'm only a quarter."

"That's enough for Hitler to put you in the gas oven."

Cameron was shocked.

Yes, Cameron has a choice. He is not a Jew by birth, not according to Jewish law anyway. He can deny this part of himself the way those of us born of Jewish mothers cannot.

Perhaps this is why so many of us see this accident of birth as a burden. But it is not. I realize today that it is a gift.

Every Jew should be proud of the extraordinary people he or she comes from. Our ancestors gave the world its conscience some four thousand years ago. Today, living in a culture shaped by the ideas of Judaism, we forget the immoral nature of some of the most sophisticated societies of antiquity. Greece and Rome were characterized by barbarism, pedophilia, killing people for sport, high illiteracy rates and grave social injustices. The justice and freedom we take for granted are of Jewish origin. They flow from the idea of monotheism — belief in one absolute God to whom all of humanity is responsible.

But Judaism goes even further than that. It is a religion based on deeds — good acts — rather than on faith alone. Unlike Christianity, which demands faith in Jesus as God as a prerequisite for salvation — so that a serial killer like Jeffrey Dahmer can find Jesus and make it into heaven — Judaism believes in advancement through merit. You gain entrance to heaven based on the life you've led as a human being, based on the acts of kindness you've performed and the commandments you've fulfilled.

There's a *lot* of them — 613. I'll give you just a few: feeding the hungry, being honest in business, being faithful in friendship, learning Torah, praying with sincerity *and*, last but not least, believing in the oneness of God.

I leave the Jews reading this book with one more shocking thought: Adolf Hitler knew what Judaism was about better than some of the German Jews living in the Third Reich. He understood very well the purpose of God's chosen people, and this is why they were threatening to him. He declared:

It is true we Germans are barbarians; that is an honored title to us. I free humanity from the shackles of the soul: from the degrading suffering caused by the false vision called conscience and ethics. The Jews have inflicted two wounds on mankind: circumcision on its body and conscience on its soul. They are Jewish inventions. The war for the domination of the world is waged only between these two camps alone, the Germans and the Jews. Everything else is but deception.

CHAPTER

TWENTY-THREE

I have to pause here to make this admission — in the last chapter I violated another little-known Jewish law, which forbids *lashon hara*. *Lashon hara* literally means "evil speech," and it pertains to the prohibition against speaking badly about your fellow. It doesn't matter if what you are saying is the truth, it's still forbidden.

Jewish law recognizes that the famous children's saying, "Sticks and stones may break my bones, but words will never hurt me," is plain wrong. Words can hurt very much. The underlying idea is that God created the world with words — therefore words have great weight and meaning — so watch what you say.

While I was studying Torah with Rabbi Aaron, he told me many interesting stories. One that stuck with me was about his ten-year-old daughter. One day she came running to him after school.

"Daddy, Daddy, a boy hit me with a spitball in school today."

"He did?"

"Yes, and he hurt me."

"What's the boy's name?"

"I can't tell you," his daughter replied. "That would be *lashon hara*."

Of course, I had no idea what the child was talking about until the rabbi explained it to me.

"Did you ever find out who hit her?" I asked the rabbi.

He laughed. "No, I never did."

Wow. Can you imagine what would happen in our society if everyone behaved like this little girl? First, people would trust each other, having no basis for suspicion. Second, all gossip would be out the window. Most newspapers would be very thin. And the tabloids would be out of business. Now *that* would make this a better world.

I must admit it is a difficult law to obey. I myself like a little gossip. Virtue is not photogenic; who wants to read about a nice guy? But there should be some limits, because gossip and rumors spread so quickly, like an epidemic. So much harm is done when millions of people are fed lies, innuendos and half-truths. A recent example is the poor security guard who discovered the bomb at the Olympics in Atlanta and then was put through hell as network news, followed by every newspaper in the country, spread the false rumor that he had planted it. It's a wonder the poor guy didn't go mad or commit suicide. Certainly his life was ruined. I hear he is suing, and I hope that he collects millions to make up for the pain he has endured. I'm a great believer in the First Amendment, but it's not there to protect irresponsible behavior by headline-hungry reporters.

One scoop that led to a tragic ending involved the trashing of an American hero, Oliver Sipple, who had saved the life of President Ford. For putting his life on the line and tackling the would-be assassin Sara Jane Moore, Oliver Sipple asked just one thing of the press: Please grant me my privacy. By the time the media were through digging up all the dirt on him — i.e., that he was gay — his family had disowned him, his mother was dead, and finally Sipple himself committed suicide.

The stuff the media reported about Sipple may have been true, but so what? He was dead.

Rabbi Telushkin has proposed a Speak No Evil Day and even got a bill introduced in the U.S. Senate, but as of this writing the measure is stalled — probably because all election rhetoric would have to be suspended for that amount of time. And aren't politicians always running for office? Is there a time that would be safe for them?

Can you imagine an election campaign without either candidate saying something nasty about the other, even for one day? I can't.

And I guess tabloid presses would be shut down that day — they would have nothing to sell. I hate to tell Rabbi Telushkin, but his bill will never pass. The lobbies against it are too strong.

Sleaze sells. It makes billions of dollars for tabloid owners every day. They may be respectable businessmen on the surface, but they are guilty of pandering to the lowest inclinations of humanity.

Of course, we have laws; if they print lies, we can sue them. And some people do. Doris Day, Tom Selleck, Clint Eastwood, to name a few, have taken the tabloids to court. But it is obvious that these rags regard lawsuits as just part of the cost of doing business.

Some years ago there was a story in the *National Enquirer* about Carol Burnett that depicted her as drunk at a dinner with Henry Kissinger. Carol was incensed. Of course, it wasn't true. She decided to sue. After lengthy and costly legal proceedings, the courts decided that she had been wronged and awarded her damages of $1.6 million. The legal staff of the rag fought and argued, and got it reduced to $200,000 on appeal.

What did Carol win? Her legal fees were over a million dollars. Imagine the time and effort expended. The public rarely sees a retraction. All the public remembers is a story about Carol Burnett being drunk.

Sometimes the stories have a kernel of truth — Carol Burnett did have dinner with Henry Kissinger and wine was served — but the little kernel of truth is twisted and exaggerated into a huge lie.

After my helicopter crash, the tabloids went to town, trying to find out the horrifying details. (One even offered the police officers in Santa Paula, where the accident happened, $50,000 for any photos of me inside the wreckage.) When they didn't get much, they just made it up: KIRK DOUGLAS NEARLY DECAPITATED IN HELICOPTER CRASH, read one tabloid headline. In Europe a tabloid reported, KIRK DOUGLAS DIES IN CRASH! Who has the conscience to make up this stuff?

And then again, who reads this stuff? Who believes it? Of course, I've never met anyone who admits buying these rags, and yet millions are sold.

A French tabloid published a long story about the breakup of my marriage to Anne. We debated whether we should sue. Would it be worth it to expend the time and effort? What would be the result? More attention to the story with a possibility of a tiny retraction?

But we decided to go ahead. And we won. A retraction was printed hidden somewhere in the back of the paper. The small sum we received in damages we gave to a French AIDS charity. Was it worth it? I don't think so.

The worst damage done by the tabloids, as far as I'm concerned, is the influence they have had on legitimate media.

There was a time that reputable newspapers — *The New York Times*, *Washington Post*, *Los Angeles Times* — took seriously their responsibility to deliver the news honestly and to deal with the important issues of the day. But now what is happening?

With modern technology and hidden cameras and microphones, is anyone's privacy protected? If you happen to be involved in current events, you might as well go live outside on a public street. Nothing of yours will be sacred, will be safe, not even your garbage.

I'm not kidding. They stole mine and showed it on national television!

Some time ago a TV show reported an inventory of the garbage in the alley behind my house. They made an amazing discovery — an empty carton for suppositories. I can't believe that these ridiculous words came out of the mouth of the young attractive reporter on national television.

This must infuriate the tabloids, since garbage is their terrain. But now they've got a lot of competition for every garbage can — who can get the smelliest garbage first?

Do we have to hear about the sex lives of our presidents? Years ago, such a topic would have been considered indecent. It was well after the fact that we learned that President Eisenhower had an affair with the woman who was his wartime driver. Franklin Delano Roosevelt would never have been elected if his illicit love affairs were known. Did these affairs interfere with their performance as president? Of course not. President Kennedy's sexual activities were practically common knowledge at the time, but they were never discussed in the media.

But that was before the legitimate media became influenced by the tabloids. Now they dig into every rumor and piece of gossip. It is getting to the point that a eunuch has a better chance of getting elected.

The sexual behavior of any political candidate should have nothing to do with the public. Did President Clinton have an affair years ago? I don't know and I don't care. That's between him and his wife. Unless he commits an act that would interfere with the performance of his duties, his private life should be his own.

The sad thing is that many decent people are staying away from national politics for this very reason. Who wants their life dissected, their family embarrassed, their friends hounded?

I once suggested to my son Michael that he take more interest in politics.

"Sure, Dad," he said, "I admire what you've done for your country. I'd like to do something — get more involved."

"Good idea, Michael . . . why don't you run for office?"

He laughed at me.

"What's so funny?"

"Oh yeah, Dad, and have them criticize me for smoking pot in college, and bring up every love affair I had and every love affair I didn't have? No way."

Come to think of it, should I be telling this story here?

Will that be a tabloid headline? KIRK REVEALS MICHAEL SMOKED POT.

Then, of course, the legitimate press will have to pick it up — what else could they do, after all — and the whole thing snowballs. Just remember what I said if, a week after reading this book, you see a distortion of it in your supermarket.

But isn't it sad?

No great man has ever led a life free of mistakes. Anyone who has, just hasn't had the guts to take risks. There is something murky in every great man's past. But if he goes into politics, it will be found out and blown out of proportion.

I think the people going into politics today are either fools or very courageous.

Two women both made widows by assassins, Mrs. Leah Rabin and Mrs. Jehan Sadat.

As I'm writing this, the civil trial in the O.J. Simpson circus is in progress. Supposedly three prospective jurors claimed that they had never heard of the O.J. Simpson trial before. If that is true, they have to be aliens from another planet because it was virtually impossible for anybody in this country to avoid it.

I took personal notice of the O.J. Simpson case ever since June 12, 1994, when I first heard that Nicole Brown Simpson and her friend Ron Goldman were murdered.

The evening before I had had dinner in O.J.'s company at a charity benefit for Bathsheba Hospital of Jerusalem. I had introduced the two honorees — Mrs. Anwar Sadat, the wife of the president of Egypt who was murdered in 1981, and Mrs. Yitzhak Rabin, the wife of the prime minister of Israel who was then alive. We didn't know that he too would be murdered. I was glad to perform this function because I had known these two women over many years, and I admired their husbands as peacemakers.

During the cocktail reception, I bumped into O.J. Simpson. He introduced Anne and me to his girlfriend, a very attractive young lady, Paula Barbieri. We talked about the time he came to my house several years before for some business meeting. It turned into a joke because neither one of us could remember why we had that meeting. Afterward, Anne remarked what a handsome and charming man he was.

And the next night his ex-wife Nicole and her friend Ron Goldman were murdered.

Since then, of course, the world — myself included — has been riveted by this unfolding drama, a soap opera delivered in daily installments. In the midst of a story that constantly crossed the line between make-believe and reality, it was sometimes possible to forget that two young people were really murdered — that this wasn't a TV drama, that this was real heartbreak.

But at least one person in the courtroom didn't lose perspective. Dominick Dunne, who was writing about it for *Vanity Fair*, had lived through such madness once before. His twenty-two-year-old daughter Dominique had been murdered by a suitor whom she rejected. The legal farce that followed culminated in her murderer getting less than three years in prison.

During the O.J. trial, Dominick was in constant demand as a dinner guest — everyone was anxious to hear the latest from someone who actually sat in the courtroom. One evening at a dinner party, I said, "Dominick, I'll invite you to dinner when the trial is over and you've run out of dinner invitations."

I admit I became addicted to Court TV. My back was hurting, and I found relief only when lying down. There are only so many things you can do when you are in bed. It was difficult for me not to watch the live coverage when the case was in session. But watching it depressed me.

Millions were being spent, most of it taxpayers' money. The prosecutors' time and energy were being taken away from other cases, as were the time and energy of policemen. The jurors were away from their families. Everyone, including the people watching, was wasting a lot of time, time in which something productive could be accomplished.

But my son Michael did not agree with me. He thought that O.J.'s guilt or innocence was secondary to what America was subliminally learning by watching the trial.

"Look, Dad," he pointed out. "This case involves an interracial marriage, and we have come to accept that. And if the black man is the villain, that picture is very well balanced by a black attorney, whose courtroom brilliance far outshines the well-known stars sitting beside him. On the other side you have another brilliant black attorney and a woman as the lead prosecutor." And then Michael said, laughing, "And the whole thing is watched over by a Japanese-American judge."

No dummy, my son. This trial, so riveting to all Americans, was giving them a picture of their own country. Leave it to Michael to find something worthwhile in this morass.

But I still wasn't convinced that the positive outweighed the negative.

The tabloids, as might be expected, had gone totally crazy over the case, and the legitimate media just plain lost their heads.

Every day during the trial *lashon hara* — evil speech — dominated the proceedings. It didn't matter if it was being printed by the *National Enquirer* or *The New York Times*, reported by *Hard Copy* or *CBS Evening News*. It was all the same trash.

My final word: You can put icing on a pile of manure, and it's still not cake.

CHAPTER
TWENTY-FOUR

While I was watching the O.J. trial I felt guilty to be wasting time. I needed something useful to do during the long sidebars, so I decided to update my address and phone book. Have you ever done that? I never had. Not until now.

So, let me tell you, if you're over sixty, think twice before you try it. And if you are over seventy, well, it's guaranteed to be just too depressing. If, for a moment, you've managed to forget about your own mortality, this simple chore will remind you — over and over again.

But my phone book was such a muddle. Some time ago, because my wife was so meticulous about keeping everything current, I had started using a copy of her book. Then my secretary added my own numbers into it, and the whole thing got commingled into one big mess. I just couldn't stand looking at the lists of the best bakeries, caterers, single women for parties, et cetera.

So, with Court TV humming in the background, lying in bed with an ice pack to ease the pain of my bad back, I decided to be productive and attack the book. I grabbed my red pen and started with A.

Immediately, I sliced through "Air Conditioner Repairmen" and "Antique Shops." I also wasn't interested in "Art Appraisers." But then I came upon "Astaire, Fred."

My heart skipped a beat. Why had I undertaken this chore? There would be so many friends to cross out.

Into my mind flashed a picture. We had taken Fred home after a dinner one night. He got out of the car, danced up the steps to the house, then across the porch, tipped his hat at the door and disappeared. Unforgettable.

It made me sad to put a line through his name, but I did, and went to the B's.

"Bathroom Fixtures" — out. Then "Blanc, Noel." I took a deep breath. Our friendship was never the same after the accident. It had been Noel's helicopter, and he had been very badly injured. Every time I saw Noel, I was reminded that two young people had died and that we had lived. I flipped over the page.

"Brando, Marlon." How the hell did he get in here? I never called him; I never even met him. I've always admired his gargantuan talents; his extraordinary performances in *On the Waterfront, A Streetcar Named Desire,* and *The Godfather* will never be matched even though, God knows, many have tried.

But talent, in any measure, is a God-given gift. If you are born with it, you have an obligation to do something in life to show your appreciation for the gift you have received.

We can all cite endless examples of extraordinary actors who have done extraordinary things for the world: Audrey Hepburn and her work for UNICEF; Elizabeth Taylor and her work for AIDS causes; Paul Newman and his fight against drugs, as well as countless contributions to many charities; Robert Redford and his efforts to help independent filmmakers through his Sundance Institute; Steven Spielberg and his support of Holocaust organizations. I could go on and on.

But what about Marlon Brando? He claimed that he had taken up the cause of the American Indian. When he won his second Oscar, he sent an actress dressed up in Indian garb to refuse it. The media took pictures of him with his Indian friends. To show his sincerity, Brando gave them a huge parcel of land. But it also had a huge mortgage which was not paid off for another year.

Later Kevin Costner made the movie *Dances with Wolves* and changed America's attitude and American film portrayal of Indians forever. It could have been the movie that Brando talked so long about making, but never committed to do.

"Earth gets its price for what earth gives us," the saying goes. Brando never wanted to pay the price. His superficial interest in causes was never backed up by real actions. It was merely a self-indulgent whim. And so he flitted from cause to cause like a bee buzzing from flower to flower, but crapping, not pollinating.

At the sentencing of his son Christian for the murder of his sister's lover — a crime that took place in Brando's home — Marlon became the star in the courtroom. The world had sympathy for the plight of this father, whose son was sent to jail and whose daughter bore the loss of the father of her unborn child. Later, in an interview with *Paris Match*, his daughter Cheyenne accused Marlon of sexually molesting her. Was this true, or was it the imaginings of a troubled girl? We don't know. But shortly thereafter, she went back to Tahiti and hanged herself.

Every family has its problems, including mine. You do the best you can. And sometimes, when tragedy strikes, you try to help others. Marlon made an attempt to help somebody else. He appeared on *Larry King Live* to bemoan the treatment of illegal immigrants, especially one Mexican woman whose beating by the police was widely publicized. In fractured Spanish he invited her to share his home. Did she have a television set at that time? I don't know. Was she listening? I don't know. Did she accept this invitation? I don't know.

Then, suddenly, he launched into an anti-Semitic diatribe against Hollywood. People, especially those who knew Marlon personally, were amazed.

The reaction to his TV interview must have startled him. He immediately recanted, saying, "I love Jewish people." He could have used the standard expression: "Some of my best friends . . ."

He agreed to a press conference to set the record straight. It was to be held with Rabbi Marvin Hier, the director of the Simon Wiesenthal Center and Museum of Tolerance. But not a pound of him arrived at the interview.

Instead, Rabbi Hier, facing the expectant journalists who had been waiting for the appearance of the actor, announced that the issue had been resolved. He related to the press that in their private meeting Marlon had cried with remorse.

I laughed. One of the best actors of this century should have no trouble crying in front of an audience of one small rabbi. Then Rabbi Hier announced, "Marlon Brando is not an anti-Semite."

I don't believe it. But I do believe he is one of the greatest actors of the twentieth century.

Well, we all suffer from something. Right now I am suffering from the effects of a stroke, and this gargantuan talent with his gargantuan body suffers from senility.

As I am writing this, it occurs to me that in the last chapter it was so easy to tell you about the law forbidding *lashon hara*. See how hard it is to follow. But then I have always been a sinner.

"Doctors." Lists and lists of them. In Los Angeles, and in every major city in the country. I'd hate to count how many of them had looked at my bad back. I kept them all in my phone book, just in case.

"Dog Trainers," maybe.

Then "Douglas, Sons."

Michael's phone numbers and addresses went on forever. His office in Los Angeles, his homes in Santa Barbara, Aspen, Majorca, New York. Then Joel's addresses and numbers in Nice and Los

Angeles, Eric's in New York and Los Angeles, Peter's in Montecito and Los Angeles.

"Dressmakers." No difficulty there; I crossed them out.

I couldn't believe the number of pages filled with information that I didn't want to know. I almost ran out of ink crossing out so many F's — "Fences," "Firewood," "Floor Refinishers," "Florists" (three pages of them — did you know there is a shop called Flowers That Bloom in the Spring? What do they sell the rest of the year?), and finally I came to a person, "Fields, Freddie."

He used to be my agent. Sometimes it seems to me that almost everyone used to be my agent. Freddie was a charming guy, but he didn't look so charming years ago when he was drowning in the Mediterranean and I dove in like a B-movie hero and fished him out. Gratitude? Forget it. Freddie was more concerned about the embarrassment. I put my red pen to work.

Now I was up to "Kitchen Appliances." Out. They were not listed alphabetically, because "Kissinger, Henry" followed them.

I knew Henry Kissinger before he was *Henry Kissinger*. We first met at the oceanside home of Joan and Tom Braden, where Nelson Rockefeller had brought him.

Henry impressed me. A Jewish immigrant from Germany who spoke with a heavy accent, he was brilliant and charming.

We became friends. Anne and I had him to our house often. His eyes bulged behind his thick

263

glasses as we introduced him to Frank Sinatra, Gregory Peck and many others. He was delighted when Anne arranged for Jill St. John to be his dinner partner. He loved Hollywood.

I will never forget the time when he visited us in Palm Springs; we stood together in the guest room as I explained to him the talking alarm clock. Of course, Henry didn't see the long wire that was attached to a ball next to my foot.

"Henry, watch this."

I addressed the clock: "What time is it?"

I secretly pressed the ball with my foot, and a computerized voice from inside the clock gave the time: "The correct time is ten-twenty-eight."

Henry was very impressed.

"Try it," I said.

Henry cleared his throat. "Vot time eez eet?"

There was no response — I didn't step on the ball.

Henry looked at me, puzzled.

"It must be your accent, Henry."

Henry was disappointed until I explained my subterfuge. We laughed.

I liked Henry. And when he got married, I liked his wife, Nancy.

One time when Nancy's mother was not feeling very well, Anne arranged for the two of them to spend ten days in our Palm Springs home.

If Henry was dazzled by the glitter of Hollywood, I was dazzled by his meteoric rise on the world political scene. Now Henry was no longer a Harvard professor. He was secretary of state, deciding the fate of this country and a dozen others. Henry was a star, much bigger than I.

I thought we were close. But a big change had come over Henry. Now when he came to California, he no longer remembered my number. He called the heads of industry. I was hurt, but I understood — he was trying to secure a future for himself after he left public office; he wanted to make his household name worth something tangible — like money.

When we ran into each other in New York, he'd ask me, "Vy don't you call me ven you are in town?"

I never did. Friendship is a very delicate thing. It needs to be nourished or it dies. Red pen.

"Kubrick, Stanley." Red pen again. We had done some wonderful work together, but a squabble over using Dalton Trumbo's name on the *Spartacus* script ended our relationship. Too bad.

My red pen kept slashing away. There were so many names I didn't remember. But then worst of all were the names of so many people who had died. I tried to be efficient and move along quickly.

But when I came to "Lancaster, Burt," I stopped. This was a name I simply would not cross out. I could not.

I tried to move on, but a heavy cloud had settled over me. I turned off the TV. The ice pack had melted, and my back was more sore than ever. Was this pain a reminder of the fragility of one's body?

So many people I had worked with were dead —

James Mason and Peter Lorre from *20,000 Leagues Under the Sea*. Sir Laurence Olivier and Charles Laughton from *Spartacus*. Rosalind Russell, Lana Turner, Ava Gardner, Susan Hayward . . . Rock Hudson, Fredric March, Yul Brynner, John Wayne.

It was too depressing. You get to a point in life where it seems your friends are falling away like leaves in autumn. I thought of the first lines of Shakespeare I learned in high school: *"All the*

Eddie Lewis, who produced my best films at Bryna, always listened to me very patiently and then did it his own way.

world's a stage, / And all the men and women merely players; / They have their exits and their entrances . . ."

Don't tell me that there isn't some force dictating who lives and who dies. Who survives a helicopter crash and who gets killed.

Rabbi Aaron told me that in the Jewish view, Shakespeare was right, the play is written — that is fate. But we are not "merely" players. We all have the choice of playing the hero or the villain, of taking an active part in the drama of life or being hapless victims of it — that is our free will.

On Yom Kippur, the Day of Atonement, God reminds us that He keeps score of what we do here on earth, what choices we make. On that day, it is written in the Book of Life who shall live and who shall die . . .

So many of my friends had died. And yet others were going strong. I flipped the book's pages and tried to concentrate on the living.

"Lewis, Eddie." My God, I hadn't spoken with him in years. He was the head of my production company, Bryna. We did a big body of work together — *Spartacus, Lonely Are the Brave, Seven Days in May* — all my classics. I should have made him a partner; maybe he wouldn't have gone elsewhere.

Was this still his number? I dialed it. His recognizable voice answered. He was bewildered but delighted that I was calling. He and his wife had just finished writing a musical that Harold Prince was going to produce on Broadway. I told him how happy I was for him.

Then he asked me what I was doing and seemed

shocked that I was studying Torah.

"You were always the Jewish goy. What made you change?"

"Eddie, when you are in a helicopter crash and two young people die, you have to ask yourself a lot of questions."

"My God," Eddie said in an awed voice. "You've become spiritual."

We made plans to get together, and I felt good when I hung up the phone.

After "Maids," "Manicurists," and "Magicians" (I kid you not), I came to "Malden, Karl and Mona."

My God, the people who knew me longer than anyone else in Hollywood! A great couple. I worked with both of them in summer stock when I was a junior in college. They helped me decide to change my name from Izzy Demsky to Kirk Douglas (Karl had changed his name from Mladen Sekulovich).

On an impulse I picked up the phone and called. Karl's voice was as dynamic as ever. "Kirk, if I had a son, I would like for him to be Michael. He's such a great guy."

"You taught him a lot when you guys did *Streets of San Francisco* together."

"Nah, all I told him was when we're saying shit, talk fast; when we have a good scene, we take our time."

I was chuckling when I hung up. I was feeling better and better.

The Q's — a short list — brought another smile

Karl and Mona Malden have known me about sixty years; we met in summer stock when I was still in college. (© *Hella Hammid*)

to my face. "Quinn, Tony." We made *Lust for Life* together, and the title of that movie would be a good summary of Tony's own story. Last time I saw him he was sitting in a restaurant with his young secretary and a beautiful little baby girl, Antonia, their daughter. Tony, eighty, was beaming like the new proud papa he was. I never found out how his wife Yolanda, an Italian spitfire, adjusted to all this.

I hope he stays in my phone book for a very long time.

"Reagan, Ronald." Didn't vote for him. Didn't call him.

We were never that friendly with the Reagans, but when Anne helped Nancy get through her mastectomy they became close. Hence the entry.

I felt sorry for Nancy. Imagine a wife living with

her husband for forty years, and suddenly he doesn't even recognize her.

The first time I heard intimations that President Reagan might have Alzheimer's was from Anne. At dinner parties, Nancy would ask her to sit next to "Ronnie." Driving home after a dinner one night, Anne ruminated, "I wonder if Ronnie is getting Alzheimer's." I waited. "He's only interested in the distant past or in a joke. He talks about when he was in movies. But never mentions his eight years as president."

Several times a week, coming out of Mike Abrums's gym, I would run into him, waiting to come in, always accompanied by two Secret Service men.

"Good morning, Mr. President," I'd always say, and we'd shake hands. "Hi," he'd reply with his usual smile, but never called me by name. I'd wonder if he recognized me.

Mike Abrums, who guided the president's exercise routine during his eight years in the White House, never discusses any of his famous clients. But one day he mumbled softly, "I don't think he remembers that he was the president."

Of course, eventually, many people caught on. And then, finally, just before the tabloids broke the story, it was made public. The president wrote a very touching letter to the American people revealing that he was a victim of Alzheimer's.

Now I never run into him going to the gym, and I never see him at dinner parties. Nancy comes alone.

The S's. After "Safes and Vaults" and "Saks Fifth Avenue," I came upon "Sinatra, Frank." He took up a lot of space. Addresses and telephone numbers in Palm Springs, Beverly Hills, Malibu. So many numbers for a guy I never called — I had known him for forty years and yet I never really knew him.

And I have to admit that I didn't like him even before I met him. It was 1946, and I was playing a small role on Broadway. After the performance each night, I looked forward to a hot pastrami sandwich, which I bought at the Gaiety Delicatessen to eat leisurely at home in Greenwich Village. But the night Frank Sinatra opened at the Paramount Theater on Times Square that wasn't easy to accomplish. I had just bought my sandwich, but the way to the subway was blocked by hundreds of screaming girls crowding around the theater hoping to catch a glimpse of him. Who the hell was this Sinatra, anyway?

He pissed me off before I even met him. Because of him my hot pastrami sandwich got cold.

Of course, Frank Sinatra was then and is now a legend. That word "legend" is used too often in our profession, but when it comes to him it really applies.

I remember his eightieth birthday, celebrated at a small, private dinner party at George and Joleen Schlatter's house. As we drove up, I looked at my watch. It was one minute past eight. "Anne," I said, "I bet you Frank is there." And he was. Frank was always punctual. For all the dinners and social events we attended together, I never remember him once arriving late.

As we sipped our before-dinner drinks, I watched Frank and Greg Peck in intense conversation. I don't ever remember talking with Frank for more than a minute or two at a time. Maybe Greg really knows Frank, I thought. I don't.

What I did know was that Frank intimidated people. They were so anxious to please him. My son Peter tells the story of one afternoon at Sinatra's hacienda watching a houseguest fawning over him.

"Where would you like to go for dinner tonight?" Frank, always the gracious host, asked his guest.

"Anywhere you say, Frank."

"Well, what would you like to eat?"

"Anything you like, Frank."

Peter grimaced. He was sure that if Frank said, "What time is it?" the guy would respond, "Anytime you say it is, Frank."

I felt sorry for the people who tried to get close to Frank. They were in a precarious position, because they never knew the mood of the emperor. You could be Frank's closest friend and then suddenly, for some unexplained reason, you were out. You never knew why.

Our place in Palm Springs was often a halfway house for the people he discarded in this way. Yul Brynner had been very close to Frank, and suddenly he was out. And Yul didn't know why. He spent a couple of weekends at our house in Palm Springs before he was reinstated into Frank's good graces. Nobody knew why he fell out or why he was back in.

Greg and Veronique Peck spent several weekends at our halfway house before they once again became part of Frank's in-crowd. Pat De Cicco was pathetic during his expulsion. Leo Durocher, man-

Frank cooks pasta for Anne's birthday party. He would never do that for me.

ager of the Dodgers, was devastated when he lost favor.

I am convinced that my friendship with Frank survived all these years because I never tried to get close to him.

My wife got along better with Frank than I did. I remember, years ago on her birthday, Frank insisted on bringing all his utensils and ingredients to our house and making an Italian feast for her that he served himself. He certainly wouldn't have done anything like that for me.

But tonight was his eightieth birthday, and I did get close to him.

Frank joined me at the bar and ordered his usual Jack Daniels.

"Spartacus," he said, "I like standing at a bar," and tapped the top affectionately. "Reminds me when I was a kid — eleven or twelve years old — trying to reach up to my father's bar."

(I always thought his father was a fireman.)

Frank took a big sip and continued. "They had a coin machine to play music and I used to sing along. They started giving me nickels, dimes and quarters, and I thought, Hey, for singing? This is quite a racket."

"I envy you, Frank," I said. "My father spent a lot of time in bars but he never took me along."

It was probably the most personal thing I ever said to him. He didn't say anything in response. Instead, he squinted at the bartender, a pleasant, middle-aged African-American who was regarding Frank with awe.

"What's your name?"

"Joe, Mr. Sinatra."

"Get a glass."

Frank insisted that the bartender pour himself a drink. They clinked glasses, and Frank wished him a happy holiday. The bartender seemed ecstatic as Frank continued chatting with him.

I've seen Frank often single out a waiter, a bus-boy, perhaps a parking attendant, and bestow on him a momentary friendship.

I tapped him on the shoulder and raised my glass: "Frank, happy birthday. Tonight, when you're lying in bed, forget all the adulation and bouquets tossed at you this week, just think what you've done since you've left Hoboken, and give yourself a pat on the back. But make sure you thank God for the great talent that He gave you, and thank Him for allowing you to use it in a way that has made a difference in the world."

I think Frank was touched but he didn't show it. It was hard to know what Frank was thinking. He always seemed to cover up his emotions with a joke. You could only see Frank's vulnerability in his songs. His singing expressed so many qualities that you never saw in him at other times.

In my opinion, Frank is a great singer because he is also an excellent actor. When he sings a song, you hear the lyrics. You feel the mood.

After dinner, Frank and I walked outside on the covered veranda. His voice was coming through the speakers, singing "The Way We Were." We looked out into the garden, and a soft drizzle was coming down. In the pale light, Frank's face looked like a little boy's as he turned to me with an impish grin, motioned with his head, and we both stepped out and looked up at the sky and let the rain wash our faces. That's the closest I ever got to Frank.

After Sinatra, I hit "Single, Men." Three pages of them. Of course some of them were no longer single and others were dead. Then "Single, Women." Another roll call of the dead. My red pen slashed through them quickly, yet so many of these names gave me an odd feeling — shadows from the past, some pleasant, some unpleasant.

"Trumbo, Dalton." I could see him now: a parrot perched on his left shoulder, his ever-present cigarette in a cigarette holder held in his mouth at a jaunty angle. I could hear his soft, emotional voice when he came to the studio for the first time in ten years. "Thanks, Kirk, for giving me back my name." How could I cross out *that* name?

"Wyler, Willy." He had died so many years ago. He had directed me in *Detective Story*. To my mind jumped the image of me carrying his pregnant wife up the steps to her bedroom. He asked me to do it because he had a bad back. I didn't know about bad backs then; I carried her up with no problem.

"Wilder, Billy." I stopped and put down my pen. Brilliant Billy. How I enjoyed doing *Ace in the Hole* with him. The friendship we started at that time endured for many years, and suddenly it ended. Why, I don't know. I must have done something wrong. What did I do to offend him? I asked but he would not respond. His friends tried to find out. They didn't know. I was confused.

I missed our friendship; I missed his sense of humor, his sardonic remarks. We would be at the same dinner party, but there would be no contact. He would be very pleasant to my wife, but ignored me.

I was baffled. Finally, I wrote him this letter:

Dear Billy:

For years, I have lived in a Kafka state, not knowing what sin I committed against you. You never told me and I tried to find out without success. But whatever I did wrong against you, I apologize.

And for the hurt with a loud silence you imposed on me, I forgive you.

Happy New Year.

He never responded.
But at least I tried. Goddamn it, I tried.

Now I was sorry I ever started on my phone book. Why didn't I just tell my secretary to clean it up? But I was too far into it to quit — I was almost finished.

And then something hit me. There were two important names missing from my book. They had never been there. Yet they were two people who meant so much to me. David Tomlinson and Lee Manelski. My two friends whom I had met for just a brief moment in the sky.

Dead like so many others that I had just crossed out with my merciless red pen. It suddenly occurred to me that very soon someone else would be doing this with my name. Gone, irrelevant, phone number disconnected.

Am I preparing for my own death? When you're approaching eighty, you finally have to recognize that death is inevitable. The daily obituaries remind you. A lot of people die *before* they're eighty! Most of the names in my book that I crossed out with my red pen had not lived that long.

Yet I find it's not frightening to think about death. Just the opposite, it can have an invigorating effect. You do your housecleaning and put your affairs in order: "Set it straight forever; better late than never." You think about what else you want to do that you haven't done yet. You sharpen your goals, and life becomes exciting again. You try to help others, you say things you didn't have the guts to say, you study Torah. It seems to hold all the secrets of life.

I look around me in amazement. Suddenly, nature seems a miracle I'd taken for granted. So, please shed no tears; I don't intend to die today. I have too many things to do tomorrow.

Last weekend I was in Palm Springs. Saturday morning, the Sabbath, I woke early. Everything was quiet in the house. I walked over to the window and sat down. I took the Torah from the table, but I didn't open it. Instead, I picked up a pad and pen and started to write:

I looked out of the window — and I saw God! Well, I didn't really see Him, but I felt His presence when the first rays of dawn's light bathed the mountain with a thin veneer of brilliant gold. What a gorgeous sight!

And slowly, as the day brightens, I see snowcapped ranges in the distance, against an aquamarine sky dotted with white, fluffy clouds that look like sheep.

I turned my eyes toward the plain — tall, graceful trees gently swaying in the breeze.

Does God love nature more than man?

Have you ever seen an ugly landscape? Never! Never!

But look at how many ugly people you see — inside and out.

Maybe it's because nature accepts whatever God gives — without complaining — that God seems to love nature more.

I need your love, God. Help me to be like a tree — weathering the weight of ice and snow, torrential rain, stifling drought and backbreaking winds. All without a murmur.

Oh God — let me be like a tree, endure my pain silently — and like a tree always reach to the heavens.

CHAPTER

TWENTY-FIVE

My studies of the Torah continued with Rabbi Braverman. I had been at it seven months now. I finally finished Genesis and dove into Exodus.

More drama and riveting stories. As this second book of the Bible begins, the new pharaoh has long forgotten how Joseph had saved Egypt from starvation. Now he feels threatened by Joseph's relatives, the Israelites, who in his eyes have become too comfortable and too prosperous in his country.

(Do we know this story, or do we know this story?)

Next the pharaoh enslaves the Israelites and issues a decree that all their newborn boys are to be thrown into the Nile.

But one Jewish mother decides to use this method of killing Jewish babies to save her son. What thoughts crossed the mind of the mother as she made a basket for her baby and put it into the very waters of the Nile that had claimed the lives of so many Jewish innocents? What heartbreak she must have endured as she watched the basket drift away.

Of course, she isn't trusting fate alone; she sends her little girl, Miriam, to follow the basket along the banks of the river. Ironically, it is the daughter of the pharaoh who, while bathing, spots the basket, rescues the baby and adopts him as her own son. She calls him by the Egyptian name *Monios* (Moses), meaning "drawn from water."

So Moses grows up a prince in Egypt doted on by the same pharaoh who had ordered his death. We know nothing of his royal upbringing as the pharaoh's grandson, because the next thing the Torah tells us is that Moses is grown up, and he takes a stroll outside the palace. This is when he sees an Egyptian beating a Jew. Moses is incensed. In a fit of temper — which is going to plague him his entire life — he kills the Egyptian.

Boy, I could sure identify with a man losing his temper.

After some Jews inform against him (What did I say? Only the Jews can destroy the Jews), Moses flees into the wilderness, whereupon he loses his temper again when he sees shepherds harassing some young girls trying to draw water at the well. (The well, the biblical aphrodisiac.)

The girls take him home — they are the daughters of a man who is also in exile — and he marries one of them, and goes to work as a shepherd for his father-in-law.

This is a riches-to-rags story. What is God telling us here?

Sixty years pass and we hear nothing more. Then suddenly, while shepherding his flock, Moses sees an amazing sight — the burning bush; it is burning, yet the fire does not consume it.

Well, we all know the rest of the story. Moses

pays a call on the new pharaoh, accompanied by his brother Aaron who does the speaking because Moses has a speech impediment. He demands, "Let my people go," and after the ten plagues and the parting of the Reed (not Red) Sea, they are free at last.

That's where the real story begins, because as these former slaves begin their trek across the burning sands of the Sinai, they are not happy campers. It's a hard journey and these stiff-necked people never seem to quit complaining. Yet Moses, the man with a temper, leads this cantankerous crew with endless patience. This man, who was a prince in Egypt, relates to his people with the utmost humility. During his time in the wilderness, he had completely remade himself. No wonder God spoke to him.

Moses became my hero. I wanted to visit the Sinai, where it all had happened. I had seen awesome pictures of mammoth rocks, scarred by wild winds, rising in the sand where nothing grows and nothing lives. This is where Moses had walked; I could almost feel the heat under the soles of my feet. I had read that the Sinai offers a view of the night sky the likes of which cannot be seen anywhere else on earth. When everything becomes pitch black, it is possible to see all the stars — the sky looks like someone spilled a salt shaker; there is not a square inch without a star in it. That is what Abraham saw when God promised him his descendants would be more numerous than the stars.

Of course, no one really knows which mountain

is Mount Sinai, where Moses received the Ten Commandments, but there are several candidates. The local Bedouins offer camel-guided hikes to the fearless who want to see the breathtaking panorama of one of the most forbidding places on earth, where my ancestors met God.

I yearned to have this experience — to reach the summit at dawn and, with my own eyes, to see stretching down below me the wilderness where Jews, my ancestors, wandered over forty years before they found what they were looking for.

Maybe I'll find it too.

Yes, I would see this incredible place. Yes, I would climb the mountain. Moses was my age when he did it. If he made it, I could too.

I told Anne, "I tell you what I'm gonna do. Go to the Sinai and climb a mountain."

"But Kirk —" she tried to interrupt.

I went on: "I'll spend the night in a Bedouin tent, and long before daybreak I'll start my climb. I should make it to the top by the time the sun starts to rise. In case my sneakers give out, I told them to have a camel standing by."

"But Kirk —" she tried again. "With your back — you will never . . ."

"Moses was my age when he made that climb. I can't wait."

My wife said nothing.

I made my travel arrangements to fulfill this dramatic quest. It took a lot of work. I planned to hire a private helicopter — yes, I was fine with that — and contacted the Egyptian ambassador for permission to fly from Israel across the Egyptian border into the Sinai.

But my wife, ever the pragmatist, insisted that I first have a medical checkup, since my back was still troubling me. With great confidence, I accompanied her to Dr. Rick Gold's office and let him take my blood and put me through many tests. Then he had me do a stress test on the treadmill. After five minutes, he stopped the machine. "Kirk, why don't you let your wife climb the mountain, and you stay here."

I couldn't see my wife's face because she turned her head away to look out the window, but the movement of her shoulders told me she was chuckling.

"Wait a minute, Doc, not so fast," I said. "They have a camel standing by."

"A camel! With your back? You're crazy."

My wife was still looking out the window.

I didn't go to the Sinai, nor did I climb Mount Sinai. Instead, my editor Ushi made the trip, and when she came back she converted to Judaism.

Let me sound a warning to Jews who hire gentile girls to work for them — make sure this doesn't happen to you. If it does, you might end up with a very efficient worker who is a constant thorn in your side, reminding you of your own failings as a Jew. Not only that, this person will be taking a lot of time off. Let me tell you.

She will cut out on Friday afternoons in the winter, giving herself plenty of time to get home before sunset — four-thirty — and get ready for Shabbat. Saturday, she will be totally unavailable, will not even answer the phone, and driving anywhere . . . well, just forget it.

And that's not all. There are so many Jewish holy days when the same rules apply. With a people close to four thousand years old, the Jews have amassed lots of occasions to memorialize.

Don't expect much work in October — the worst month for holy days, with Rosh Hashanah, Yom Kippur, Sukkot, Shmini Atzeret and Simchat Torah all following in quick succession. Just write off October.

Then, of course, she will only eat in kosher restaurants. Thank God, in Los Angeles we have many of them, but if you live in San Francisco or

Ushi was a great editor before she converted to Judaism.

Baltimore or someplace like that, you have a problem.

Now, the nice thing is that she will invite you for Shabbat meals at her home, where you are likely to meet a dozen or so fascinating people who will engage you in deep, stimulating conversation. (Idle chitchat and talk of work are not appropriate on Shabbat.) They will sing inspiring songs, and you will go home feeling somehow different. And the next Shabbat, if you are not invited, you will feel something is missing. My solution is to go play golf.

Of course, it's not easy to be converted to Judaism. First of all, we Jews don't proselytize. As a matter of fact, a candidate for conversion is turned away three times before he or she is accepted into a course of study that — in an Orthodox conversion — takes a minimum of a year.

When Ushi began this process after her first trip to Israel, I thought surely she would give up. But she stuck with it. I couldn't believe it. I didn't encourage her. As a matter of fact, I tried to hold her back. But after sixteen months of intense study, she knew more about Judaism than I did. That was embarrassing.

Why couldn't she have remained a brilliant gentile working on weekends, when I liked to do most of my writing and editing? Oh, no. How was I to know that her soul was searching? How was I to know that the research she was amassing to help me was answering her own deepest questions? How was I to know that in my quest to find more meaning in

286

Judaism, she was the one who actually found it?

When she returned from the Sinai, the date for the final ceremony — June 23, 1995, or, if you want to get technical, the 25th of Sivan, 5755 — was set. I was perplexed when I stood with three rabbis at the Los Angeles Mikvah. The convert must pass an oral examination at that time and then immerse herself in the water of the *mikvah*.

One of her friends took pictures. In them, we see her radiant face looking up from the water. Everyone is singing and smiling. I'm the only one standing there with a grim face.

For her Hebrew name, her rabbi suggested Uriela, after one of the four archangels. Michael is the guardian angel, Gabriel is the angel of strength, Raphael is the angel of healing and Uriel is the angel of light.

I would still call her Ushi.

While my editor became the angel of light, in a coincidence too symbolic for comfort, I became the devil in a music video called "The Garden of Allah."

Here's how it happened:

My son Michael telephoned me one morning. "Dad, how would you like to work with Don Henley?"

"I'd rather work with you."

"I know, Dad. Me too. The script is in great shape, and as soon as I finish *American President*, we'll set a shooting schedule."

"Great, Michael. I can't wait."

"But about Don Henley —"

"Who's that?"

"Dad, are you kidding me? Don Henley . . . you know, of the Eagles?"

"Doesn't ring a bell, but I used to live on Eagle Street when I was a kid."

"Bad joke, Dad. The Eagles were a famous rock group some years after Rudy Vallee."

"All right, wise guy."

"Seriously, Don is doing a music video for his latest single, and he wants you to play the devil."

"Did you say the devil?"

"Yeah — in a music video for MTV."

"He wants me to sing?"

"No, you have to lip-sync to his voice."

"Michael, that sounds ridiculous."

"Listen, Dad, he's a brilliant guy. Will you talk to him?"

It's hard to say no to my son. So I spoke to Don Henley, and I have to admit, I was very impressed. He had written a song based on a book — must be a first — *The Death of Satan: How Americans Have Lost the Sense of Evil* by Andrew Delbanco.

He explained to me that the message of the song is that in our world, good and evil have become

I am the devil in an MTV video for "The Garden of Allah," sung by Don Henley. (© *1995 Geffen Inc.*)

confused. Once upon a time we knew what was evil — the devil had a name and a place to hang his hat, so to speak. But today we don't have an adequate name for evil, and we don't know where to locate it. Evil simply weaves itself into the fabric of our society.

Pretty heavy stuff. All this from a rock singer. I was amazed.

He called the song "The Garden of Allah" after a now-defunct Hollywood hotel that, during its heyday in the 1940s and 1950s, was the site of orgies, drunken rages, bloody brawls, divorces, suicides and murder.

The project was interesting, but me on MTV? I just couldn't see it. Don Henley was insistent. Finally, I think I was won over by his appeal to my ego — that I was the only one who could play the devil. Come to think of it, should I have been insulted by that?

I did it, even though it was difficult to lip-sync to the unorthodox rap beat with which Don Henley speaks as the devil.

During the filming, my bad back attacked me with a vengeance. I lay like a lemming on a couch between scenes. When it came time to put on my devil outfit — a seersucker suit and red wingtips — I couldn't even tie my own shoes. Then they had to transport me to the set in a wheelchair. Was God telling me something?

But I did it. And I enjoyed it. The devil I played was an elegant fellow who was upset that he had become obsolete, yearning for the good old days when good was good and evil was evil. I recited these lines with great intensity, thinking of current events:

Today I made an appearance downtown
I am an expert witness, because I say I am
And I said, "Gentlemen . . . and I use that word
  loosely . . .

I will testify for you
I'm a gun for hire, I'm a saint, I'm a liar
Because there are no facts, there is no truth
Just data to be manipulated
I can get you any result you like
What's it worth to ya?
Because there is no wrong, there is no right
And I sleep very well at night
No shame, no solution
No remorse, no retribution
Just people selling T-shirts
Just opportunity to participate in the pathetic
  little circus . . .
And winning, winning, winning."

I saw the finished product on MTV, and I gotta say, with all the dream sequences and the smoke of hell, I hardly recognized myself. Maybe nobody else did either. Suffice it to say that so far no one has asked me to do another music video.

CHAPTER

TWENTY-SIX

"Pain is God's megaphone to wake up a deaf world," said C. S. Lewis.

If that is true, then I was stone-deaf. Over the four years since the helicopter crash, I had experienced pain in intricate variations. Somehow I felt that God was telling me something, and I was not responding. The pain was mostly bearable, but it could take on different forms, requiring different reactions.

Often sitting for an extended period of time — like through dinner — was not a pleasant experience. I found relief by lying on the floor, which I did many times — even at the homes of friends — while others chatted over coffee. Driving two hours to Palm Springs presented the same problem. I would travel in a station wagon lying down on a mat while my wife drove.

The pain seemed to have a mystical quality, coming suddenly, undulating in waves of varying intensity. It would begin in my back, then travel down my right leg. This, I learned, is the sciatic nerve tract — the same part of the anatomy that was affected when Jacob wrestled with the mysterious stranger in the night. When the struggle was over, Jacob was left with a permanent limp but was blessed with a new name, Israel — one who had struggled with God. To this day, Jews don't eat the sciatic sinew of any animal.

My wife kept telling me, "Don't read too much into it. The only thing God is telling you is that you are getting old."

Maybe, but I thought otherwise. And it took me a long time to come to this conclusion — my life was spared in that helicopter crash because there is still some mission that I must fulfill. But if this was so, why was God making it so difficult for me to get around? Or, was He reminding me that on the good days, when I felt no pain, I wasn't getting on with the program?

After an unpleasant episode lasting several days or sometimes a couple of weeks, I would feel better, be back to normal. The pain was there, but at a level that nurses call "discomfort," which means bearable. I'd go out to golf again. I was happy, hitting the ball well — for me, a 21 handicapper. And then I'd hear the megaphone of God blasting my eardrums.

In the fall of 1995 — just when the story hit the front page of the *Hollywood Reporter* that *Song for David* was listed for a spring start and a Christmas 1996 release — I began to experience a totally new kind of pain. Real pain. The kind of pain that does things to you — makes you depressed, makes you angry, makes you cry.

I had run a gauntlet of chiropractors, acupuncturists, hydrotherapists and physical therapists, but nothing helped. Dr. Goldstein felt that at my age a lengthy operation would be too risky. I had to keep trying noninvasive alternatives.

He did think that an epidural might help. This is when they stick a needle into your spine and inject it with medication. "Anything," I said. It didn't take long. I lay on my belly, my eyes tightly closed, hating the thought of a needle going into my spine, but I didn't feel anything because they first give you a shot of anesthetic. Afterward I felt much better. I had planned to go to Fillmore to work on my book with Ushi, so I asked him if he thought I could go, and he said, "Oh yes, you will be fine." My driver took me to my destination. I was feeling good.

Then, in the evening, the anesthetic that had accompanied the epidural wore off, but the epidural medication did not kick in. Suddenly, I was hit with an avalanche of pain. Lying down was the only position that seemed to alleviate my suffering. So I went to bed.

But now I was trapped. Every time I tried to sit up, such excruciating pain would hit that I couldn't even go to the bathroom. I lay in bed for twenty-four hours — my only comfort a urinal. I didn't know how I would get home.

Ushi called Dr. Goldstein, and he prescribed a Demerol injection so I could get up long enough to get into my car and be driven to a hospital. It was Sunday, but Ushi got the prescription filled at a local pharmacy. Fortunately, among her many talents, she is a licensed practical nurse, something that came in very handy that weekend. The

Demerol helped and I was driven straight to Cedars-Sinai.

A few days in the hospital brought the pain to a manageable level — which is to say I could get out of bed to go to the toilet. But nothing the doctors did eliminated the pain completely. Besides, I wasn't sure that the doctors had done anything, really. Maybe the pain subsided on its own just as it had before. And maybe it would come back with even greater intensity as was its wont of late.

My son Peter suggested I check out the UCLA Pain Control Center. Pain control — that sounded good to me. They started me off with two epidurals in my back. These had about as much success as the first one — none. Then they gave me a series of oral medications to relieve the pain. Success rate? None.

I must say that they began each treatment with great optimism — optimism that I could not share because the pain was still there. Their next course of action was narcotic pain patches. You peel off the back of a two-inch square plaster patch and slap it on your chest. One day I had two patches side by side. I felt sleepy because the narcotics were making me drowsy, but I couldn't sleep because the pain kept me awake.

Lying on my side in bed with a pillow between my knees, the only position that brought relief, I was subjected to one sadistic commercial after another touting TV's answer to back pain. They would show a man grimacing from pain just like me, holding his back just like me. And then the magic salve, ointment or potion was applied or consumed and — eureka! — there was this man all smiley-faced, free from pain. As the announcer extolled the charms of this or that concoction, we'd see the former sufferer happily dancing, skiing or playing tennis. Oh, sure. Don't waste your money.

My pain seemed to be worse in the morning. I would get out of bed, lower myself to my knees because I could not stand up, and crawl on all fours to the bathroom. While needles of pain raced up and down my back, I'd struggle into the shower to let the hot water pound away at the soreness. Sometimes the pain would abate for a bit, but more often than not my day would depend on how much willpower I had to walk around while still in pain.

I became very depressed. Enduring the pain was depressing enough, but the thought that I could not make the movie with Michael in this condition really sent me into the dumps.

For New Year's we went to Palm Springs, and there the pain attacked me with savagery. Everything that had come before was just a rehearsal for this.

Doctors came from the Eisenhower Hospital. First they put a morphine pump in my arm, with a nurse coming over periodically to replenish the dope. Then one of them hit on the idea of implanting a catheter into my back — to deliver the anesthetic right to the site. At last, someone with brains, I thought. Soon it will be over.

The nice doctor promised that very shortly I would be free of pain. I waited tensely. After a while, I had to go to the bathroom. I ignored the urinal; this would be the test. I stepped out of bed, and my left leg folded under me like a broken umbrella. I realized that I had lost all sensation in my good side — it had been put to sleep by the anesthetic. The bad side — the right side — still hurt like hell. The anesthesia pump was pumping all right — but it was either implanted in the wrong place, or the nerve tract was so blocked that the medication was going where it wasn't supposed to go.

I had been in unbearable pain for nearly two weeks, and I didn't know how much more I could take. Dark thoughts entered my head — like how you get Dr. Kevorkian's phone number. And this is not a joke.

Then I remembered the autobiographical novels of Henry Roth, author of *Call It Sleep* and *From Bondage*, which he wrote when he was in his eighties.

He writes that he asked his devoted wife to frame an inscription of two Greek words for the wall of his study. "What do they mean?" she wanted to know. He put her off with, "Just a couple of words. Happen to be meaningful for me."

The words he wanted to hang on the walls of his study were *Apothanein thelo* — "I wish to die."

At the time, he was in constant pain with rheumatoid arthritis. Nevertheless his literary output was amazing. How could he wish to die when his talents were so vibrant? I became angry with Roth, yet I identified with him. I shared his joy and his suffering. There is a time in each of our lives when we wish to die, but we can't give in to it. Not when you are still creative, productive, and can do some good! No, no, no — never!

Dr. Goldstein finally agreed — and a myogram confirmed — that my only hope was an operation. We had reached the point of last resort.

My friend Lord Hansen flew me in his private plane from Palm Springs to Los Angeles, and I found myself once again at Cedars-Sinai.

I knew this was a risky operation — I wasn't at all sure I would make it. And I was scared.

Maybe I am more religious than I realize, because as I lay on the operating table and began to feel the effects of the anesthesia, I recited: *"Shema Yisrael Adonai Elohainu, Adonai Ehad"* — Hear, O Israel: the Lord our God, the Lord is One! This has been the Jewish cry for thousands of years, recited three times a day by the observant. These were the last words uttered by Jews entering the gas chambers of the Holocaust. This is a prayer that every Jew must recite before he dies.

But I lived. Not only that — the operation was successful. The excruciating pain in my right side was eliminated. There was still some pain in my back, but it was entirely bearable. I was very grateful to God and to my doctor, Dr. Goldstein, a wonderful man.

After the operation, he told me a very touching thing. He said he had admired me as an actor for many years — the heroic roles I played made me a giant in his eyes. When I came to him as a patient he could hardly believe it. Here was the lion himself. Well, during the operation, taking out the bony spurs that were pressing on sore nerves in my back, he felt like he was taking a thorn out of a lion's paw.

I liked his story. But I didn't feel much like a lion, moving around with the help of a walker. "Be patient," Dr. Goldstein scolded me, promising it would all change very soon if I would only follow a strict physical-therapy regimen.

Boy, would I!

And he was right.

Within days, I graduated to a cane, and in less than two weeks' time, I surprised even myself by walking around the living room with no support.

I was on my way to a complete recovery, and Dr. Goldstein was promising me that it wouldn't be long before I was back on the golf course.

I didn't care about the golf; all I cared about was that my ailments would not interfere with the *Song for David* shooting schedule. For the moment, all systems were go.

I couldn't wait.

CHAPTER
TWENTY-SEVEN

After only two weeks of intense physical therapy, I went outside for the first time and walked to the corner and back. What an accomplishment!

To celebrate, Anne arranged for a manicurist, Rose, to come to the house and give me the full treatment. Meanwhile, Anne left to console Barbara Sinatra, who had fallen down a marble staircase and hurt *her* back. She was now wearing a brace.

It was late afternoon. I reclined in my chair, eyes closed, hands extended as the manicurist buffed my nails to perfection while I bragged about my walk to the corner.

Suddenly, I felt a strange sensation, a buzz making a circular path around my right cheek. It didn't hurt. I started to tell Rose about it, but I couldn't speak. Only incoherent babble came out.

Rose, who had been a nurse in Israel, knew immediately that I was having a stroke. She yelled to my housekeeper, "Concha, get Mrs. Douglas."

Concha ran into the room and, seeing her boss slack-jawed and babbling, went into hysterics and started slapping me as if to bring me to my senses. I could feel her slaps, but they were not helping me.

They reached Anne at Barbara Sinatra's, and she immediately called Dr. Rick Gold, my internist.

"Can he walk?" he asked.

"I think so."

"Then get him into a car and bring him down to the hospital — much quicker than sending an ambulance."

Dr. Gold met me in the emergency room together with my friend Dr. Goldstein and Dr. Colin Stokol, a neurologist. The first thing they said was, "Show me your teeth." And, perplexed, I did. Of course, I didn't realize that what they saw were all my teeth on the left side of my face, and a drooping mouth on the right.

They sent me in for a CAT scan; an MRI was out of the question because I had a pacemaker. Later Dr. Gold told me that he was relieved when he saw me walk down the corridor to the CAT scan room — he knew that my side was not paralyzed.

At no time did I feel pain from the stroke, just an enormous frustration that I couldn't speak. When I tried, all that came out were incoherent sounds.

I found myself in my old hospital room. They stuck a needle in my vein attached to an IV pole to keep liquids in my body and to infuse blood-thinners to dissolve any clots. (As I later learned, undissolved clots following surgery can cause strokes; the other major cause of strokes is a burst blood vessel in the brain.)

Needless to say, I didn't sleep that night. All I kept asking was, "God, why me? What did I do wrong?"

But no answer came.

Two weeks earlier, I had left this hospital, and now I was back. I hated this place where you are helpless, dependent on nurses and doctors who seem much too pleasant.

A speech therapist came into the room to test my swallowing abilities. I had not been allowed to eat or drink anything because they didn't know if my esophagus was affected; if it was, I could choke on my food. But now she said it was okay for me to try it. The first foods they let me have were mushy things.

I was not a good patient. I complained every day, "I want to get out of here," except that it came out "Ash one t'gut o'har."

After four days, they said I was in good shape, except of course that I could barely speak and the right side of my face drooped; when I smiled only the left side lifted up. They said the stroke I had suffered was very mild. All I needed was rest and lots of speech therapy, and I would be back to normal in short order. So I went home, and I think the hospital was glad to get rid of me.

Now I had to deal with what I came to call "my double whammy."

There seemed to be no time in my day when I wasn't seeing a speech therapist, a physical therapist, a back doctor, an internist or a neurologist.

If I was not momentarily concerned with my speech, the residual pain in my back or leg reminded me that I still had other problems.

For fifty years I was an actor who could walk and

talk. But am I an actor now? I asked myself. How can I be an actor if I have difficulty walking and difficulty talking? What am I?

I would be alone in my room when such dark thoughts would come upon me, and suddenly the tears would start to flow. I'd feel silly but I couldn't stop them. Sometimes I castigated myself for giving in to self-pity. But at other times, I wasn't even sure why I was crying. I just felt a deep sadness. Then I read in *Toward a Meaningful Life*, a book by the late Rabbi Menachem Mendel Schneerson:

> Have you ever just burst out in tears for no apparent reason, finding yourself in deep sadness? That is the soft voice of your soul, crying out for attention, asking to be nourished with at least as much care as you nourish your body.

Was that happening to me? Was the "soft voice" that of God shouting into my ear through His megaphone? Why couldn't I decipher the message?

I cried and prayed.

At other times my depression turned to anger. I was mad at everything and everybody. I was mad that this thing had happened to me. And most of all I was mad at God.

At those times, my prayers became diatribes directed at heaven. "How could You do this to me?" I cried. "Just when I was in the middle of studying Your Torah!"

I didn't hesitate to argue with God, because I knew that Abraham had argued with God. If he could do it, then as his descendant, I could also. They say you can plead with God, you can argue with God, but the worst sin is to ignore God.

Well, there was no danger I would do that.

"Hey, God, count all the things I've done to help the Jews. Didn't I give a speech about Judaism at the Synagogue for the Performing Arts? Didn't I give two more speeches in Glasgow and London? So why can't I speak now?"

I ranted and raved, presenting all the reasons why I didn't deserve this fate. Sometimes I thought, maybe He just doesn't like me. But then, I was reminded that He did spare me in the helicopter crash, and I was back to square one. What did God want from me?

I was like a child learning to talk, and it was a humbling experience. I never realized the complexities of speech.

It seemed like such a simple thing. I had been using it for over seventy years. Then suddenly it's taken away from me. Dr. Gold tried to explain to me that a small part of my brain on the left side of my head, which controls the muscles of the cheek on the right side of my face, was affected.

I had to learn to speak all over again. I had to relearn innumerable combinations of movements of tongue and lips and breath control to re-create the sounds of speech I had previously taken for granted.

Speaking is nothing short of a miracle. You realize this only when you can't do it.

Did you know that "k" and "g" sounds are made the same way in the back of the throat, as if coughing, except the "g" has a vibration. "N" is made by flattening the front of the tongue against the roof of the mouth. "F" is made by biting your lower lip with upper teeth. "R" is made by growling and biting with your teeth. "J" is made by keeping your back teeth together and showing your front teeth.

If you consciously had to think of that, you wouldn't be able to talk. And that's just *letters* — let me tell you about *words!*

Have you any idea how difficult it is to say a simple word like "stop"? The "s" is formed by blowing air across the top of your tongue. The "t" is formed by the tip of your tongue touching the roof of your mouth.

You don't know how long it took me to get the connection of the "s" and the "t."

I had to train for hours. Like a boxer trains in a gym, I had to train my mouth. Over and over again.

S s s s s s s . . . top . . . stop
S s s s s s s . . . tove . . . stove
S s s s s s s . . . teve . . . Steve
S s s s s s s . . . tone . . . stone

And on and on and on, until I felt like a complete idiot.

And that's just *one* combination of sounds.

After two months of this torture, I had not yet caught up to my granddaughter Kelsey's speech, and she was only three years old. But I refused to give up.

One of the worst things about being a victim of a stroke is that people feel sorry for you. They want to do things for you. And since you also feel very sorry for yourself, you are more than willing to accept their gifts of kindness.

Your wife says, "Would you like something to drink, honey?"

"Yes, that would be nice."

"Don't get up, sweetheart," she says, "let me get it for you."

And why not? You've been through a lot. You deserve this loving attention.

Beware of such temptation. Don't let yourself give in.

Such well-meaning people are encouraging you to become an invalid. Next thing you know, they'll be feeding you and diapering you like a simpering idiot. You can't let them.

I found myself fighting a growing dependency on my wife. "No, honey, I'll get it myself. And while I'm up, would you like a drink too?"

A small thing, but it means a lot. When you do that, you feel stronger. You have accomplished something. That's how you cling to your willpower, and you need every ounce of your willpower to get better.

I realized that I could not give in to the temptation to become a sedentary child tended by others. I had to take control. I had to will myself to get better. I had to fight for it.

People have to learn how to deal with you. My wife had to make a big adjustment. The best thing she did was forbid me to complain. When I would declare morosely, "Anne, I'm not speaking well today," she'd answer, "Oh no, honey, you're just temporarily out of order."

But, three months after the stroke, I had to face the fact that I was still not speaking well. Frankly, I had believed that by now I would be reciting sonnets from Shakespeare. Instead, I still had a difficult time enunciating words, and to be understood I had to speak very slowly.

Then Michael called. He asked how I was doing. And I tried to answer him, but he couldn't understand my garbled speech. "What, Dad? What, Dad?" he kept saying.

In exasperation, I said, "Don'... you... spik... Englees?"

Of course, that got a raucous laugh out of him — and me.

"Listen, Dad, you just keep working with your speech therapist, and we will make that movie yet."

"Michael, why don't you go to a speech therapist," I stammered, "and when you talk like I talk we will do the movie together and no one will know the difference."

We hung up laughing.

I felt better.

Laughing is very good for you, I discovered. Norman Cousins, who died of cancer, wrote in his book, *Anatomy of an Illness*, that laughter has healing power. Dr. Ni, my Chinese acupuncturist, agrees with that. He said that he has a statue of a laughing Buddha at home, and it reminds him to do something silly every day.

So I tried it, and it seemed to help me. I came to like playing the role of the clown. My right lip sagged, giving my face a contorted look, so one of my best lines became, "I can't say that with a straight face."

Now my face has straightened out, so I can't use it anymore; besides, there is no one in town who hasn't heard it.

With all that I did make progress. And then came the great day when at last I surpassed my granddaughter Kelsey. Cagily, I asked her: "Kelsey, can you say 'transcontinental'?"

She couldn't.

I left her in the dust. Now I was with the six-year-olds.

All right, smartass, you're laughing? Let me hear you say the following quickly:

> *All I want is a proper cup of coffee*
> *made in a proper copper coffeepot.*
> *You can believe it or not*
> *but I just want a cup of coffee*
> *in a proper coffeepot.*
> *Tin coffeepots*
> *or iron coffeepots*

are no use to me.
If I can't have
a proper cup of coffee
in a proper copper coffeepot,
I'll have a cup of tea.

When I'm in a restaurant, I may have difficulty ordering a meal. But when it comes to coffee, boy do I shine.

I pause and read what I have written. It sounds so cute, clever and funny. But I don't feel cute, clever and funny — I am scared. I have been telling jokes, doing my physical exercises, working with my speech therapist and trying to write a book. And suddenly I am tired, the pain returns in my back, it's difficult to walk, my speech doesn't seem any better and I feel like I'm drowning in a morass of self-pity. I know I shouldn't give in to this feeling, but I don't give a damn. Woe is me. I want to give up. I want to sink beneath the surface of the earth and disappear.

Then I pick up the paper and read a story about Jean-Dominique Bauby. He was a French journalist, a bon vivant, a father, a man half my age, and he had a stroke too. It left him paralyzed from head to foot. He had control only over his left eyelid. They asked him to blink if he understood and he blinked — his mental faculties were intact; he was victim of the locked-in syndrome. Totally imprisoned in his body, he learned to use a coded alphabet and dictated a book by just blinking his eye. The book became a huge best-seller in France.

I put the paper down and say to myself, "Why don't you shut up, Kirk."

CHAPTER

TWENTY-EIGHT

Two months after the stroke — when I was still speaking like a three-year-old, when I was still declining dinner invitations from friends, and when the news of my stroke had not yet made the papers — I was forced to make my handicap public.

I had to get up onstage before a theater audience of three thousand and a worldwide TV audience of a billion, to accept a special Oscar for lifetime achievement.

The announcement had come a few days after my back operation, and I had cheered myself by working on an acceptance speech that would be short and amusing, yet poignant. The stroke canceled that.

I asked my son Michael to accept for me, but he said, "No, Dad. I won't do it. You should have gotten an Oscar forty years ago. This is your moment. Go up there even if you have to crawl."

For a while it looked like I might have to do just that. But as I graduated from a walker to a cane to walking by my own power, at least I felt confident that I would not have to crawl.

My speech therapist assured me that by the time the Oscars rolled around, I would be speaking perfectly. And so I began to work on a shorter speech.

I stood in front of the mirror and tried to practice saying, "This old man was lucky. Lucky to know such talented and magical people — my friend Burt Lancaster, Gene Kelly and so many more who brought excitement and joy to a troubled world . . ."

But my reflection in the mirror looked like Dr. Jekyll or Mr. Hyde (I forget which was the ugly one).

I sounded so incoherent and looked so bad with my droopy face that I decided the less the audience saw and heard of me, the better. I'd get up there, say "Thank you," and leave the stage.

On Oscar evening, we arranged to have the driver bring me to the stage door about a half-hour before I was to go onstage. An escort brought me into the office of Quincy Jones, the show's producer; I could wait there in private. Oprah Winfrey was also waiting there. She looked ravishing. I could not resist mumbling, "Oprah, if I was thirty-five years younger, you wouldn't have a chance." I think she understood my garbled speech, because she laughed uproariously.

And then it occurred to me that I had not yet seen Steven Spielberg, who was to present my Oscar. I asked Quincy, "Is Spielberg here?"

"Yes."

"Where?"

"You'll meet him onstage," he said, chuckling at my insecurity.

Another escort came to guide me through the crowded backstage area, where pandemonium reigned as scantily dressed dancers raced to change costumes and crews moved scenery between segments of the show. I was given a chair in a quiet spot in the wings where I could await my entrance and watch on a TV monitor what was happening onstage.

Whoopi Goldberg, the M.C., came over and gave me a kiss, and Mel Gibson shook my hand, reminding me that we once shared a chiropractor — I guess he's done too many stunts too.

But still no glimpse of Spielberg. I had been very flattered that he would be my presenter, especially when Quincy Jones told me that Steven had turned down presenting the Best Picture award. That made it even more meaningful. So where was he?

The face on the monitor startled me — it was me, age thirty-two, adeptly skipping rope as the boxer Midge Kelly. In quick succession my whole career flashed before my eyes — young Kirk slashing and shooting his way through life.

I felt a soft hand on my shoulder, and I looked up at the beautiful face of Sharon Stone as she bent down and kissed the old Kirk. Then I turned back to the monitor to see young Kirk kissing Lana Turner. What was make-believe, what was reality?

And then I heard a disembodied announcer's voice. "Ladies and gentlemen, Mr. Steven Spielberg."

I was relieved.

He made his entrance from the other side of the stage, and began:

" 'The dark has a life of its own.'

Kirk Douglas said that in *The Bad and the Beautiful*, one of the best movies about movies ever made.

We're celebrating and honoring Kirk Douglas tonight because he's done nearly everything on film. He's directed, he's produced, and, in the process, he's helped hammer the blacklist to pieces. And, of course, most memorably, and most lastingly, he's acted. He's done that the way he does every-

I was honored to have Steven Spielberg
present me with the Oscar.
*(Applied Network Solutions, Inc.
Rancho Cucamonga, CA)*

313

thing . . . with grace and courage. Whether he's dealing with a character onscreen, or with the all-too-real effects of a recent stroke, courage remains Kirk Douglas's personal and professional hallmark. Most stars of his stature are shaped with mythic clay. Kirk Douglas never chose that. He doesn't have a single character that makes him unique. Instead, he has a singular honesty, a drive to be inimitable. That's what animates all his roles, from Spartacus to Vincent van Gogh. There's a single thread drawing all his characters together. It's called conscience. Every person he ever played had one. And, because Kirk Douglas never made his characters simple. No good guys or bad guys. He shaded heroics with self-doubt, shaped his villainy with compassion."

He had figured out my secret philosophy of acting — when you are playing a strong character, find his weakness, and when you are playing a weak character, find some part of him where he is strong.

"His characters weren't bigger than life. They were life reconverted, something we all could identify with, something that would touch us out there in the dark . . . something that gave the dark a life . . . and a light . . . of its own.
Let us all welcome Mr. Kirk Douglas."

I gulped, overcome by his words. I stood up — there I was, a weak character trying to be strong. I braced myself and strode on the stage pretending to be Spartacus.

I embraced Steven as he handed me the Oscar — it was much heavier than I thought. Then I turned to the audience. Wow, thousands of people filling the tiers of the theater all the way up to the ceiling, applauding, cheering, standing up . . . for me.

My last scene from *Champion* flashed through my mind. Midge Kelly, battered out of his senses, says to his trainer, "Didn't you hear them, thousands of people cheering for me! For me!"

And then, after the applause subsided, I peered into the audience and found my four sons sitting together with my wife. I pointed to them: "I see my four sons — they are proud of the old man." People laughed. They understood what I was saying. I went on. "I am proud too — proud to be a part of Hollywood for fifty years." I raised the Oscar. "But this is for my wife, Anne — I love you." I was startled by the tumultuous wave of applause that greeted a man making a declaration of love to his wife of forty-two years. I felt good and I raised my hands in a symbol of victory. "Tonight I love all of you, and I thank you for fifty wonderful years."

Wow! I could speak, be understood and even get applause!

With my arm around Steven, I walked off. The audience was still applauding.

They whisked me out the back elevator and to my car. I got home in time to watch the last part of the awards, and waited for my family.

Sitting there with the Oscar in front of me on the coffee table, I suddenly thought of Lee and David. Lee would never be sitting like me admiring that international trophy for aerobatics he coveted, nor would David ever win the novice championship he had been preparing for. Suddenly, it all seemed so meaningless compared to the greatest treasure of all — life.

It was late when the jubilant group tumbled into the house. Anne, Michael, Joel, Peter and Eric. Mounds of caviar and bottles of champagne were

The family holding up Anne and the Oscar.
(© Alan Berliner)

consumed. Joel, who loves to sing, led everyone in "Got a Whale of a Tale" from *20,000 Leagues Under the Sea*. It was during the making of this picture that Anne and I ran off to Las Vegas one weekend and got married — in 1954!

My last memory of the evening was of my sons and me all clinging together on the couch with my wife sprawled out on our laps clutching the Oscar; a photographer snapped the memorable moment.

To bring the evening to an end, I used my usual routine. "Fellows, they are waiting for me at the disco and I have to leave." With that I got into my pajamas while the boys all left to attend the Oscar parties that were just heating up all over town.

I picked up the Oscar, brought it into my wife's room, and placed it on top of the television set. "Don't you want to put it in your room?" she asked.

"We settled that years ago — in Munich," I replied.

She laughed.

Back then, when I was nominated for *Lust for Life*, I was the hands-down favorite. Everybody thought I would get the award. So did I. The night of the Oscars I was in Munich making *Paths of Glory*, and the paparazzi were camped in the hotel lobby waiting to catch the smile of the winner. But Yul Brynner won for *The King and I*. And quietly the photographers went home.

Alone in my room, I was one disappointed actor. I couldn't sleep. And then there was a knock at the door. The concierge handed me a package. It was a small statuette from my wife and son Peter with this

Leah, the mother of Steven Spielberg,
is much younger than her son.

inscription: "TO DADDY, WHO RATES AN OSCAR WITH
US ALWAYS . . ." (Anne had left instructions at the
hotel to deliver it in case I didn't win.)

Since then, *that* Oscar has been in my room. He
is slightly tarnished by now, but he still stands
proudly on my desk, staring at my ancestors on the
wall opposite him. I always told Anne that if ever I
did win a real Oscar I would give it to her.

It took a hell of a long time, but at last I was able
to keep my promise. And there he stands in her
room. He will never be in mine and he will never
gaze at my ancestors on the wall; that privilege is
reserved for the first Oscar — small, light, with the
gold paint chipped off in places, but still the one
that counts.

I turned out the lights in my room and went to
bed. Was it my imagination, or were the patriarchs
over my head smiling? I slept peacefully that

night. I didn't even have any pain in my back. I dreamt of Steven Spielberg.

I never knew Steven very well. We have never had dinner together, though occasionally we were present in the same room at various functions. Once we discussed — through letters — his directing *Something Wicked This Way Comes*, a Ray Bradbury story I wanted to make into a movie. He was interested, but it didn't work out. Too bad; he would have made it a hit. Once we met briefly in Las Vegas at the National Association of Theater Owners convention, where we both got awards for what I don't remember. I was fascinated by the work he was doing, filming the survivors of the Holocaust. I sent him a letter of support. So our relationship was largely confined to the U.S. mail.

In fact, I have had much more contact with his mother, Leah Adler. She is a slim, vivacious person who runs a kosher restaurant in Los Angeles called The Milky Way.

I eat lunch there often. When I come in, we greet each other with a big hug. Of course, this is against the Jewish law of *shomer n'gia*, but what the hell, we are sinners.

You'd never guess Leah is seventy-seven because she exudes the impish charm of a seven-year-old. She skips around the restaurant in Peter Pan outfits, sometimes with bells around her ankles, landing on her haunches so she can squat down and talk to her seated guests face-to-face. "Don't get the barley soup — no salt — it's dull."

I told her, "If my wife ever divorces me I will

marry you." She giggled. But it's not a bad idea. Think of it — then I would become Steven's stepfather, and he would have to take care of me in my old age. (He has more money than Michael.)

Leah never brings up her famous son, but if you cue her — "When did Steven first show moviemaking talent?" — she's off. The story that I love best was when, as a high-school student, Steven was making a home movie that called for an exploding cauldron. She bought a case of canned cherries in heavy syrup, opened them up, and then, as instructed by "the director," splashed them all over the kitchen for the explosion shot. The cherry juice never came out of the woodwork. She didn't care.

But then Leah is the woman who said to little Stevie, "Who needs to be older than ten anyway? In our family, the only rule is, Don't become an adult."

It's easy to see that Spielberg followed that rule in so many of the movies that he made, like *E.T.*, *Indiana Jones*, *Close Encounters of the Third Kind*, *Jurassic Park*.

But it is also easy to see that Spielberg became an adult when he made *Schindler's List*.

The Talmud tells us that the exploration of life should start at the beginning of the second part of life.

I started my exploration, my inventory, much later than that, not until about age sixty-five, when I began writing my autobiography, *The Ragman's Son*. But Steven Spielberg was right on schedule. His inventory took place at age forty-five, the midpoint of life.

I wondered what Leah thought of the transformation. She answered me with glistening eyes. "Who would have thought that this would happen to that six-and-a-half-pound blob?"

She handed me a *New York Times* article detailing the opening of *Schindler's List* in Germany. She became almost serious — she could never completely succeed at that — as she pointed with pride to a quotation from Spielberg and read: "As a Jew, I had to make this film."

She looked at me. "Can you imagine he said that — 'as a Jew . . .' "

As a Jew, I felt that *Schindler's List* had the greatest impact on me of any movie I've ever seen. It is already a classic. The ripples it has sent out will be felt around the world for many years to come. There is no doubt that only a man like Spielberg could have made this movie. This was a subject that many filmmakers had discussed for years. The billion dollars that *Jurassic Park* brought in and the millions that his other films earned gave Steven the power, as he put it, "to make the telephone book" if he so desired.

No studio would give the green light to a black-and-white movie over three hours in length dealing with the Holocaust — unless Spielberg was going to make it. He took no salary, setting aside all profits to charities related to the Holocaust. When I saw the movie, I was stunned. My body tingled when I heard a chorus of children singing

"Aufen pripichik . . . ," a little tune I remembered singing as a child with my mother.

It seemed to me that I was holding my breath during the entire film. When it was over, I left the theater quietly, drove home, went into my room, threw myself across the bed, and sobbed.

I cried tears of rage against all the people who had abused me for being a Jew. I became again a little boy going home from Hebrew school and running the gauntlet from block to block as kids taunted me — "Jew boy," "kike," "yid," "sheeny" — threw stones, and beat me up. I felt a surge of hatred; at that moment I wanted to kill them all. I pounded the pillow.

I got up from bed, wiped my eyes, and wrote Spielberg a note:

Dear Steven,

You deserve all of the success you have had with your films. It gave you the power — you always had the talent — to make *Schindler's List*. What a movie! A historical piece of film.

I am now in the process of writing my fifth book — not a novel. Here I try to grapple with what it means to be a Jew. You, much younger than I, have wrestled successfully.

I only have four sons. I think I'll adopt you, too.

With much affection . . .

And then he replied:

Dear Kirk,

I thought those twelve nominations gave me a boost through the roof, but your letter pushed me all the way up into the plumbing!

By the way, consider me adopted. I love making you proud.

It's nice to have a pen pal.

CHAPTER

TWENTY-NINE

Little did I know that I would be doing more business with my pen pal very soon.

It began when my literary agent, Alan Nevins, the partner of the late Irving Lazar, said, "Now that you're so Jewish, why don't you write a children's book with a Jewish theme?"

I thought, Why not? I've been carrying a child inside my belly for over seventy years. Let Issur write the book.

It didn't take me long. I wrote a story, which I called *The Broken Mirror*, based on the friendship of two boys whom I had introduced in my first novel, *Dance with the Devil*. I read it over and said to myself, Hey, Kirk, this is good.

Since it had a Holocaust theme, I sent it to the expert, Steven Spielberg, for his evaluation. He responded:

> It is absorbing and touching, and a book to be read and enjoyed by youngsters and their parents alike. In fact, it's a story which grips your attention and has so much to say in such a concise form that it should not be limited to Jewish readers.
>
> Kirk, you've done a great job. Your

agent was right to suggest you write the book!

Meanwhile, all good wishes for an early publication date.

I think it's safe to say my pen pal liked it. I decided to donate all the proceeds to his Visual History of the Shoah Foundation.

My agent made a deal with Simon & Schuster to publish the book. Liking my mother's angel stories, which I had incorporated into *The Broken Mirror*, the publisher asked for another children's book, perhaps something from Jewish folklore.

Could I become a children's author?

Yeah, I could.

I had grown up a lot, but at heart I never ceased being a kid. An actor has to be because acting is such a childish profession. An actor can't succeed in his craft if he doesn't retain a great deal of the naïveté of his childhood. Businessmen, stock-market analysts and especially politicians — it's hard to imagine what they were like as children. They are so caught up with the nitty-gritty business of succeeding that they are very far removed from their childhood. Even when politicians mention children, they seem to be referring to people alien to them.

But actors are much closer to childhood because they do what kids do when they play — pretend. Can you imagine "grown-up" businessmen playing cowboys and Indians? Burt Lancaster and I had no trouble.

The Kabbalah, the mystical interpretation of the Torah, likens the evil inclination of man to a foolish old king who is afraid of getting off of his throne. But the good inclination the Kabbalah likens to a child, because a child makes life an adventure. A child is curious. A child is not afraid to learn and to explore.

Of course, I sometimes fear that in all my eighty years, I haven't learned much. Like the lines I spoke as Spartacus, I am still asking the same naive questions: Where does the wind come from? Where does the sun go at night? I am embarrassed to tell people that — while everybody is navigating the Internet and popping in CD-ROMs — I am still trying to figure out how the telephone works. I can't get over that when it rings in your house, and you pick it up, your voice instantaneously travels, zipping along a wire to someone's ear thousands of miles away. I don't understand it.

The other day I was in a friend's private plane, and I saw him talking on a cordless telephone. We were speeding at over five hundred miles an hour, forty thousand feet above the ground, and he was talking on a telephone that was not attached to anything. I wanted to take my hand and run it around the phone to see if I could interrupt the voice that is going through the air, through the hermetically sealed cabin and then through endless space, finally connecting with someone God knows where. How could that be? I mean, I marvel at such feats of magic.

I am still that little kid who tried to get to the

other side of the moon. I remember walking home and watching the moon shining above me. I'd sprint forward, trying to race ahead of it, and look up only to see that it was still hanging there in front of me. The moon was making fun of me, playing a game. I couldn't understand why I could not get to the other side of it.

The world is still full of wonders to me. The adults around me seem to know all about it, so how come I don't? But maybe they are just faking.

I'm sure that they don't really understand the biggest mystery — the mystery of the soul. No one can answer me when I ask: What is it inside of ourselves that guides our lives? Where does that inner voice come from? What is the source of the yearnings that urge us to reach beyond ourselves?

When I bring up such questions in "polite company," I am often told to get down to reality.

But what is that? What is reality?

Reality is that we are like ants, crawling about in a vastness that is incomprehensible. Above us is the sun, bursting each second with the force of millions of atom bombs. Below us is a roiling foundation that spews volcanoes and shakes all our material possessions with earthquakes, hurricanes and tidal waves. But even the earth and all the planets are only specks when one considers what we know of the enormity of the universe. And yet we do not know what the universe is and where it begins or ends. In the limited knowledge we possess, we are like the people in 1492 who did not know that the earth was round.

We thought we would have it all figured out when we got to the other side of the moon. So we did, and still we are befuddled. We are about to travel to Mars, have a robot collect soil specimens for analysis. It will only take ten months to go there, and about the same time to get back. We seem to be planning journeys farther and farther away from earth. But maybe we are going in the wrong direction.

We seem to be avoiding the greatest, most mysterious and perhaps most dangerous adventure of them all — exploring the great unknown within ourselves.

Each one of us has to make it on his or her own. Somebody on TV can't tell you where to go. The rich and the famous cannot define it for you. They have lost it themselves long ago. And yet if you spend time in their company, you put on their glasses and, like the boy with a piece of the devil's mirror in his eye, see the world in a distorted fashion, with things that don't matter seeming large and important, while the things that are in fact precious appear as small, far away and out of focus.

The TV hypnotizes us, lets us lie in a stupor, until the day when the earthquake hits, the power goes out and we are left to confront ourselves, count the wasted hours and mourn what we cannot bring back. Only then reality looms large and clear. Until the power goes on again . . .

It took me so long to figure out that I need not go very far, need not fly to the ends of the earth, need not reach the other side of the moon, need not climb Mount Sinai even. Why did I place so much importance on that trip?

The journey is a journey into our souls. The destination has been predetermined for each one of us. The destination is death. God will decide when we have arrived. That part is out of our hands. But we have the free will, the choice, of how we travel, just how we will climb that mountain of life.

This is the message of Jonah and the whale. The Bible tells the story something like this: God asked Jonah to do something to help his fellow man. But Jonah said he'd rather get away from it all and go on a cruise. But then a storm came up, and Jonah was thrown overboard and swallowed by a whale, or, to be more accurate, a big fish. The storm, Rabbi Braverman explained to me, represents the troubles we have in life, and the big fish is the big sleep — i.e., death. But then the fish spat him out on the shore and God gave him a second chance. It's what you might call a near-death experience.

I am like Jonah. I too have ignored God's megaphone and seen some troubles in life. I too was swallowed up by a big fish that spat me out — that was the helicopter crash. God gave me a second chance to make that journey within. You won't catch me taking any cruises. I am committed to helping my fellow man — through building playgrounds and writing books — and to becoming a better person.

I don't know any quick ways to do it, but I am working hard to improve in simple ways. When driving a car, I make a point of giving the other guy the right of way. It feels good to wave somebody ahead of you, and sometimes they raise their hand in friendly acknowledgment. And when I get behind another car that is going too slowly, I try to put myself in the other driver's seat. Maybe he has a problem. This makes me less impatient, and, in the end, what have I lost — thirty seconds? If I make such an effort, by the time I get to the office, I feel better and my interactions with other people are more pleasant.

That's what I've learned in life. It might seem minuscule, but it is important. Take it slow, think before you speak, and, above all, consider the other guy, and all of a sudden the world seems a gentler place.

It has been ten years since I wrote my autobiography, *The Ragman's Son*. I am not the same person now. Only ten years have passed, but the questions that forced themselves upon me during this time — Why did you survive? Where are you going? — have reshaped me. It is only in the last few years that I have begun to discover myself.

Today, I am eighty years old — what other discoveries lie ahead?

December ninth — the morning skies opened up, pissing rain. Anne had planned a "surprise" party for 140 people and she was worried that the downpour might deter the crowds. But by seven o'clock the rain ceased. Now don't get me wrong,

I'm not saying that I have the inside track to the Man Upstairs. That's just what happened.

But certainly the One who parted the sea for the Israelites could easily stop a drizzle in Southern California to impress a doubting Jew.

It was also the fifth night of Hanukkah. That somehow seemed significant. Hanukkah is the festival of lights, commemorating a miracle. As I lit the candles I thought back six years to my helicopter crash when two young people were killed, and I said a prayer for David and Lee. But I am alive. And that is a miracle.

Still, reaching eighty frightens me. The Talmud says that it is the age for greatness and heroism, so expectations of you are high. At seventy-nine, you are still a young fellow, but by eighty you are the age at which Moses climbed the mountain, met God

Happy Birthday to the old man: "He's eighteee!!"

and gave the world the Ten Commandments. You have to know *something* by eighty. But I still felt far from being a wise old man imparting knowledge to others.

As I told you before, I don't like birthdays — I hate birthday parties — it all depresses me. Still, my wife went to a lot of trouble, so I tried to enjoy myself. The band played loudly, people were drinking copiously and my four sons were singing "Happy Birthday" in a tone that would never get them a part in a musical. I looked over the gathering, saw smiling, friendly faces. I had to admit, it was a wonderful evening.

At midnight, an exhausted octogenarian arrived home with his wife and sons. We looked at a pile of presents in a room filled with flowers. Too late to open them. I left my family in the den discussing the party, and went to bed.

I turned out the light. I could hear the murmur of the voices in the next room, but I couldn't make out what they were saying. I stopped hearing them as I became wrapped up in my own thoughts. Gee, maybe I am somebody. Maybe I have done some worthwhile things in life. But is it all over at eighty? As I pondered this question, my eyes drifted over to the shadowy figures of my ancestors on the wall. The one I could see most clearly was Moses with the Ten Commandments. It was an epiphany. No one can stop me now. Last year, they prevented me from climbing Mount Sinai, but now I am eighty, the same age as Moses, and I *will* climb that mountain.

I felt good savoring the image of me on top of the mountain looking out across the Sinai. I looked good up there. There was a breeze caressing my hair. It was a wonderful picture. Charlton Heston would have been green with envy. I glanced over to the wall again, and the light had changed so that I could no longer make out the figure of Moses.

And with that my mood changed. Why am I such a ham actor, dreaming up heroic roles to play? If I did climb the mountain, I would be disappointed if God didn't give me some stone tablets. I laughed at myself and suddenly the truth struck me. It's not important to reach the top of the mountain. What is important is the climb. All of life is climbing the mountain, even if we take different routes. But the journey is far more important than the destination, because it is of our making. What counts is how we behave as we are climbing.

When I fell asleep the last thought in my head was, Keep climbing.

Epilogue

Each morning I wake up in my study with the Chagall lithographs of my ancestors peering down on me from the wall next to my bed.

I blink my eyes and guess the time, then turn to the digital clock to see how close I've come. I'm rarely far off, but on occasion I hit it on the nose, and I feel a surge of power — I'm at the top of the morning. Then, I turn away from the clock and just lie there and pray.

I thank God for giving me back my soul, which, Judaism teaches, leaves our bodies during the night while we sleep. I thank Him for opening my eyes to see a new day as the early-morning light gently sneaks in through the curtains. It is deliciously quiet.

Once a month, the early silence is interrupted by the sharp ring of the telephone. The pacemaker test from the New York office. I get a cheery: "Are you ready, Mr. Douglas?"

And then I open the testing kit, put on each arm bracelets marked left and right, which are connected to a small machine. "Place the receiver on the machine and count to thirty," the voice says.

Then I place a magnet over the pacemaker implanted in my chest and count. I lift the receiver to my ear. "Okay?"

"That was fine, Mr. Douglas. Have a good day."

I am always amazed that the beat of my heart travels three thousand miles over the wires. That test is only done once a month, but I don't like it because it reminds me of my mortality and, more importantly, because it interrupts my peaceful morning. That is my time alone.

Everyone else is asleep — my wife, Anne, in her room next door, and even my dog, Banshee, in the kitchen.

I stretch out in my bed and test my back. Not bad. I get up and put on a robe that our housekeeper, Fifi, who has been with us for thirty years, gave me on my eightieth birthday. Then I put on my sheepskin slippers, a gift from our newcomer, Concha — she has been with us for only twenty-five years.

I leave my room quietly, turn off the night lamp in the living room and head for the front door, reminding myself to turn off the alarm. I think back to years ago in Amsterdam, New York, when no one even thought of locking anything.

I open the door and a gentle, cool morning air greets me. I touch the *mezuzah* on the doorpost and bring my fingertips to my lips. I used to think that we were supposed to kiss the *mezuzah*, but I learned that we touch it and bring our fingertips to our lips in order to breathe in the words on the tightly wrapped scroll that rests inside. It says:

Hear O Israel: the Lord our God, the Lord is One!
You shall love the Lord your God with all your heart,

with all your soul and with all your might . . . And you shall bind these words as a sign upon your arm and they shall be a reminder between your eyes . . .

That's a reference to *tefillin,* a reminder of a Jew's relationship to his God. I remember wrapping these straps of leather, which look like a harness, around my arm. I still have them in my closet, but I haven't used them since I was fourteen years old.

And you shall inscribe them on the doorposts of your house . . .

Well, I've done that.

If you will harken to my commandments, I will send the rain to your land in its time . . . so that you may gather in your grain, your wine and your oil. And I will give grass upon your fields for your cattle . . .

For a long time, I thought that this was such an anachronism — a prayer that was meant for Jews thousands of years ago, when they were living in tents tending their goats. But then I made an amazing discovery. Fruits, cereals, oils and wine don't come from a supermarket. Rain has to come in its time somewhere or we don't eat.

But take care lest your heart open itself to temptation and you turn astray, for then the wrath of God will blaze forth against you. Now that used to scare me, but not enough.

Having recited the words of the *Shema,* I walk down my driveway to pick up the newspapers. Often I am annoyed. They throw *The New York Times* close to the bushes, and it gets wet from the sprinkler. This has been going on for some time. I asked the delivery boy to throw the papers on the other side, but some problems in life are never solved.

I quickly pick up the newspapers, wave to a jogger who is passing by, and return to the warmth and peace of my bed. I unfold the paper and look at the front page: THREE ISRAELIS SHOT . . . WAR IN BOSNIA ESCALATES . . . CLINTON HAMMERED BY GINGRICH . . .

Hate, war, bloodshed — every morning.

I have given up on my generation, but then there aren't too many of us left. I have also given up on my kids' generation, the baby boomers. What have we jointly done to make this a better world? Very little. But I am an optimistic guy, and so I place faith in my grandchildren's generation. Maybe they will succeed where we have failed.

That's why the playgrounds are so important to me. When children play in harmony, they learn how to create a harmonious world. We need it so badly. We are living at a time when people haven't learned to get along with one another, in Africa, Ireland, Bosnia and especially the tiny spot called Israel. I think this last place is the key because it is a sacred place for Jews, Christians and Moslems. If people can learn to get along in the Holy Land, they will be able to do it the world over. But for the time being people continue to hate and kill each other there and everywhere. In many homes, children learn intolerance, hate, racism at the dinner table. Maybe playing in some small park, they might unlearn those things. I know it's a very tiny hope, but I have no other solutions.

The other morning I woke up with a strange feeling. It wasn't pain I felt. Not the physical pain in my back, nor the emotional pain over my awkward speech. I felt something else. I felt afraid.

At sundown today, Yom Kippur would start. Tonight I would attend the Kol Nidre services, beginning this holiest of holy days. That Day of Awe, when God writes in the Golden Book of Life who shall live and who shall die.

What fate will be waiting for me?

Would I die in the next year? Or would I be worthy of living for another three hundred sixty-five days.

Quickly, I took mental inventory of my good deeds, trying to build up my case for a good verdict. But I was still afraid.

I was afraid of hearing at the end of services the piercing cry of the shofar, the ram's horn, which emits a sound that is like no other. It is not musical and it is not discordant. It is more like a cry from the soul, responding to the sealing of its fate.

I got out of bed, and suddenly I decided to do something I hadn't done in sixty-five years. I put on my prayer shawl and the new *tefillin* that Rabbi Braverman had given me. I felt awkward and embarrassed as I sat at my desk by the window. I felt a little trepidation that one of the housekeepers would walk in and see me and think: What a funny old Jew.

But I dismissed those thoughts, and looked out of the window. Staring back at me was a nude statue of a girl that I had bought years ago in Yugoslavia.

Maybe this was the wrong setting, I thought. Never mind. I raised my eyes over the wall and bushes and concentrated on the sky. Do I really believe? I tried so hard to pray. Does anyone really hear my prayers? I don't know. But a voice inside of me said, Keep on praying, and I felt better when I had finished.

I am eighty years old. I can't believe it. As I write it down, say it and think it, it is hard for me to realize that it is reality, that I am not playing the part of an old man. I look back at everything that has happened to me, the movies that I have made, the books that I have written, especially my autobiography, *The Ragman's Son*, where I first tried to get a look at myself, where I tried to vent all my anger and resentment for not getting a pat on the back from my father. How petty it all seems now. King Solomon wrote, "In the morning, you grow up like the grass. In the evening, you are cut down."

So between morning and evening, what has happened? Within that comparatively short period of time, what have I done?

I see how all the different elements come together, how, throughout the years, they have all played their part in bringing me to this place and time.

It seems as if only now I really know who I am — my strengths, my weaknesses, my jealousies. It is as if all of it has been boiling in a pot all these years, and as it boils, it evaporates into steam, and then you look into the pot and ask, What is left? Just the stuff I started out with in the very beginning.

Issur, the little kid at 46 Eagle Street, the little kid leaning on the fence in the wintertime, before the whistle blows and the mill workers rush for home, the little kid, dreaming, wondering what will happen in his life. Where will he be years from now? What country will he go to? What people will he see?

Well, this is it, Issur. You have come a long way from 46 Eagle Street, Amsterdam, New York. You have come a long way from your mother's kitchen. Remember sitting there when your sisters were off to school, asking your mother all sorts of questions? "How was I born, Ma?" Remember what she told you?

She told me that I arrived on this earth in a beautiful gold box delicately carved with fruits and flowers and suspended from heaven by thin silver strands.

My mother was in the kitchen baking bread one sunny winter morning, when she thought she saw something outside. She rubbed the frost from the window, peered out, and saw a gold box shimmering in the snow. Quickly throwing a shawl around herself, she rushed into the yard, opened the gold box . . . and there I was! A beautiful baby boy! Naked and happy and smiling. She picked me up very carefully and, holding me close to her bosom to keep me warm, brought me into the house.

And that's how I was born. I know it's true, because my mother told me so.

When I first heard this story, my concern was for the gold box. "But, Ma, what about the box, the gold box with the silver strings? What happened to it?"

"I don't know. When I looked out the window again, it was gone."

"But, Ma, why didn't you grab the box and keep it?"

"Son, when I found you, I was so happy that I couldn't think about anything else."

I was disappointed that my mother had let the gold box disappear. But I was also very happy, because I was more important to my mother than even a beautiful gold box with silver strings attached to it, going all the way up to the sky. From then on, I always knew that I would be somebody.

But maybe it wasn't just a fairy tale that she made up. Maybe she was telling the truth and there *was* a gold box. Maybe we are all, in a sense, born in a gold box with an opportunity to do something in life.

Carl Jung said that part of our struggle on earth is to recognize the royalty in ourselves. I think when we do, we can also recognize the royalty of others. That is the secret of "love thy neighbor as thyself."

We are all born of royalty, in a gold box, even a ragman's son. Within us is a tiny seed of godliness — the Spirit of God, the *Shechinah* — and throughout our life we must learn to nourish it. Obey the voice within — it commands us to give of ourselves and help others. As long as we have the capacity to give, we are alive. It demands that even while you're hurting you can still notice that another person hurts too. It has nothing to do with age. Old people become too absorbed with themselves — with their illnesses, diminishing capacities — and stop giving of themselves. But when you stop giving, you die. To be able to give — not just money, but something of yourself to another, your love, your understanding — that is life itself.

If we adhere to that credo, we will die as we were born — as royalty, taken back to heaven in a gold box on silver strings.

So now, my only hope is that I live out my remaining years worthy of going back where I came from — in that gold box with silver strands leading up to heaven.